DOUBLE TAKE

DOUBLE TAKE

Kathryn Cole

Stoddart

Published in 1995 by
Stoddart Publishing Co. Limited
34 Lesmill Road
Toronto, Canada
M3B 2T6
Tel. (416) 445-3333
Fax (416) 445-5967

Stoddart Books are available for bulk purchase for sales promotions,
premiums, fundraising, and seminars. For details, contact the
Special Sales Department at the above address.

Canadian and Publication Data

Cole, Kathryn
Double take

ISBN 0-7737-2905-4

1. Cole, Kathryn. 2. Intercountry adoption –
Canada – Biography. 3. Intercountry adoption –
Philippines – Biography. 4. Interracial adoption –
Canada – Biography. 5. Single mothers – Canada –
Biography. I. Title

HV875.58.C3C6 1995   362.7'34'092   C95-931158-0

Cover Design: Tannice Goddard, S.O. Networking
Computer Graphics: Tannice Goddard, S.O. Networking
Printed and bound in Canada

The names of some of the people in this book have
been changed to protect their identities.

*Stoddart Publishing gratefully acknowledges the support of the Canada
Council, the Ontario Ministry of Culture, Tourism, and Recreation,
Ontario Arts Council, and Ontario Publishing Centre in the
development of writing and publishing in Canada.*

For my mother and father,
Elva May and Arthur Lloyd.
It's a small thing to give in return,
but this book is yours, with love.

MOTHER'S SONG

If snow falls on the far field
where travellers
spend the night
I ask you, cranes,
to warm my child in your wings.
— Anonymous, Circa 700 AD

CONTENTS

ACKNOWLEDGEMENTS

The nicest thing about having a book published is that it presents the opportunity to thank people who had a helping hand in it. In a book like this, those who helped create the story and those who supported its writing are easily muddled. To the characters on the following pages, and to the many others who are not mentioned but who were involved, my deepest thanks. Two major players must be acknowledged separately. "Emilia" whose name has been changed, but whose ebullient character is unalterable, was a kindred spirit long before our first meeting. Now, years and hundreds of letters later, we are truly blood sisters. Sandra Scarth was there to help when the story began and was here to assist again at the end of its writing. Without her unwavering conviction that, above all else, belonging is the right of every child, there would have been no story to tell.

So many people have encouraged my writing that it is impossible to list them all, but a few must be named. Special thanks to Leona Trainer, who suggested that this book be started and insisted that it be finished, even when I would have stopped. Her friendship and trust in me is a rare and valued gift.

And thanks are overdue to Jack Stoddart and John Denison for their generous support of my writing from the beginning.

Don Bastian and Lynne Missen, besides being enthusiastic

about the manuscript, lent considerable editorial skill in order to shape a better book. I have been very fortunate to have had their help so close at hand.

Micaela Gates was picked to be first reader with good reason. I knew I could count on her honesty and insight, as I have so many times before. It was her response that gave me the courage to show this to others. Thanks to Barb McIntyre, Pamela Coutts, Sheila Dalton, Jack Bond, and Lisa Herman — all special friends who supplied healthy doses of encouragement.

To Carolyn Jackson, who refused to let me submit this manuscript without first casting her eye and editor's pen over it, my sincere appreciation. The fact that she is my sister, friend, mentor, backup system, travelling companion, and co-conspirator earns her a special place on this page and in my heart. Thanks go to my brother Jason, for living up to the promise he made when he was only eight, even though I wouldn't have held him to it. And thanks to Christopher Jackson for keeping family trees, traditions, and ties, because he understands their worth. For my mother and father, there are no words to express my gratitude. From you I have taken far more than I was entitled to. And because of you I learned that giving birth to babies requires no special talent. But raising sons and daughters who believe they were born under lucky stars says something very special about their parents. I have always known I was one of the lucky ones.

And to Lienne and Miguela, my own beautiful girls, thank you for braving this journey with me. Your pride and willingness to share our story indicate that, in spite of everything, you sense good fortune, too. You are blessed to be from two worlds, one familiar, one veiled in mystery. Somewhere, I know, there are others who share my love for you, and who would very much like what I have been privileged to see. To them I owe an unpayable debt.

DOUBLE TAKE

1

"ARE YOU WAITING FOR A BABY?"

Terminal 1 at Pearson International Airport was hardly the place to have a baby. But there I was, unnoticed by all who passed, facing the stark reality that finally the waiting was over and motherhood was hard upon me. Only my own family, closely huddled around me, was aware that this was the moment. Strangers milled around us with glazed faces, on their way to meet someone else. They had no part to play in welcoming my child, yet fate had chosen to send them to this place, at this time. Their presence was irritating. This was intensely personal and was supposed to be private. The intruders slid past, sneezing, smoking, chatting, laughing, oblivious to us and our situation. As I watched them weave by, I feared at any given moment one stranger's eyes might focus on me. Realization of what was happening would dawn and immediately, magically, a crowd of gawkers would form, greedy to own a piece of this memory. But it didn't happen. They would forget my face, though I would remember each of theirs forever.

It was as if I was looking through a kaleidoscope that was turning in slow motion. Time simultaneously slowed down and sped up, and someone had turned off the sound. I was thinking in pictures without words. The clock above us marked 8:43 p.m. The monitor mounted close by indicated the safe, on-schedule arrival of CP flight 80 on this, surely the hottest and longest day of my life. August 27, 1980, had become the delivery date I had been working towards for so long — off on my due date by only two years — making this five-year gestation period far longer than even a couple of pachyderms would need. I deserved a place in the *Guinness Book of World Records.*

Another cramp took hold. Not the contraction kind, but the grinding kind. My innards had been complaining all day. If any one of those idiots who had blithely claimed I was having a baby "the easy way" had walked by right then, I would have made them eternally sorry.

Though I had imagined this scene many times, it had never in my wildest dreams been quite like this. Who in their right mind would picture having a baby at the top of an escalator under a sign marked "ARRIVALS"? Looking down at my feet, I found strange comfort. They might be lacking arches, but there they were, faithfully braced in front of me as I leaned against cool concrete, still holding me up, ready to step forward joyfully, or turn and run, or carry me home in despair. Whatever message the brain at the far end had in store for them, they would obey, as they always had. The floor under them was gritty with summer dust and I desperately wanted to call for someone with a mop. Everything should be shiny and clean for this.

Even as the reality of my present situation was pushing all but the last stubborn remnants of pessimism away, I tried to prepare myself for another of fate's cruel tricks. I wanted to believe this time, but for me right now, belief was dangerous. If disappointment was the only thing to get off this plane tonight, I was still determined to hold on to that small, cold lump of resolve deep inside me, so that tomorrow or the next day I could start over again. My tiny internal piece of steel was already engraved with names: Korea, India, Bangladesh, Barbados . . . Kim Chee, Baby Laura, Infant Ryan . . . I would simply have to find room on its surface for more.

I stood, pinioned from four directions. My mother on the left and my sister on the right had leaned my back against a pillar and were buttresses on either side of my body. My own feet, well in front, formed a triangle slanting back to locked knees. Together we were probably stronger than any architectural form in the airport. Even so, alternately holding my breath and puffing, I began to panic. Why had I let anyone come if there was even a remote possibility of disaster? I had tried weakly and stupidly to talk my family out of this, but of course I hadn't had a chance. Naturally, whatever was about to happen to me would happen to all of us; it always worked that way. My dad stood off to the right. My brother, Jason, and my nephew, Christopher, were beside him, no trace of doubt anywhere on their eager twelve-year-old faces.

"What if she's not on the plane?" I muttered to my sister.

"She's on it. This time it's real. You would have had a phone call if anything had gone wrong."

My father, steady as a rock, had opened the door as I arrived home from work that day with the obligatory celebration drink in his hand. It, along with several others, disappeared while chips, peanuts, and cheese did the rounds. The heat was oppressive, which accounted for the first two drinks. The third was for courage. On any other day it would have finished me off, but today I felt no effect at all. Dad made one more phone call before we left. The flight was still on time. "Let's go! Everybody in the car," he said, and out we all filed.

At the front door of the house my mother stopped me. "Try to slow everything down from this moment on. You deserve this night, and I want you to remember all of it, down to the last detail."

"I will," I promised, and I have kept my word. But there has been so much.

The terminal wall facing us now was of glass windows and doors that had been blocked with brown paper to prevent anyone seeing through to the baggage claim area. There must have been a good reason for this, but it escaped me. More people were gathering, getting in the way, coming between us and the door that had to swing open sooner or later. My sister rubbed my hand and offered encouragement, while Mom kept a firm upward pressure on my bent left elbow. Despite her outward calm, I felt her tense when the door opened and the first of the weary travellers emerged, dragging her suitcase on squeaky wheels.

As the door closed, people strained to see around its edge, anxious to catch sight of an awaited loved one. Again and again the door swung back and forth, while we waited endlessly for the face we had never seen. Gradually, the outward flow of people slowed, then trickled to a stop. Greeters drifted away, leaving us all but alone. I looked at my sister. "They didn't make it," I whispered.

"They must have. Look." Carolyn pointed to three remaining groups much like ours. They too were leaning, waiting, whispering, looking bewildered. Four babies had been promised on this flight. We looked at the three other recipient families. One man was carrying a little girl about four years old on his shoulders. She was obviously a previously adopted child, perhaps from India or Bangladesh.

"Are you waiting for a baby?" he asked.

I nodded.

"So are we. It's our second time. Do you know the escort — Mary Jane?"

"No, I don't even know what she looks like," I replied.

"Well, we do. She brought our first baby to us," he said, rolling his eyes upward to indicate the little girl up top.

"Daddy, I have to peepee," the child complained. Someone giggled and the man answered, "I can't take you now, sweetheart. Hold on. We don't want to miss the baby come out." The little girl didn't answer.

The door opened again and one more straggler emerged. The man with the child on his shoulders moved forward in time to peek inside. "There's Mary Jane," he yelled. And then the most wonderful, jubilant words I'd ever heard: "She's got four!"

My knees buckled as Carolyn and Mom hoisted each side. The child sitting on her daddy's shoulders began to howl loudly and the man beneath her groaned. I tore my eyes from the door just long enough to see a huge stream of urine spreading down and across his back, turning his beige shirt brown. The little girl was handed down to her laughing mother, while her father assured her it wasn't her fault.

The wail of that child became tangled up with the child's voice within me. *Where am I going? How did this happen?* The voice was frightened, almost panicky. There was no time to comfort or even say goodbye to the little girl who had been me. Her voice died as she slipped away and disappeared, mercifully leaving me, at long last, ready to care for someone other than myself. She didn't really need any explanations. She knew full well how we had come to this and how much I wanted to be here. Hers was less a cry of betrayal than it was a way of asking, *How did you get here? Are you ready for this?*

In that moment, oneness ended. I loosened my grip on that hard internal lump of steel and let it fall away too. It wouldn't be needed anymore. There would be no more names to scratch onto its surface. My hands and arms were empty and free, ready to reach out and hold my own baby at last.

The door opened slightly, fell back once, and then, with a stronger push, it swung wide. The grin on my face was spreading, all awareness of cramps, heat, and strangers gone. My obedient feet had received the long-awaited signal and were carrying my body bravely forward to meet my daughter.

2

THIS MUCH FUN I COULD
HAVE BY MYSELF

How all this happened was as much a part of me as breathing.
There was never a time when I didn't know I would have
children. Oh, there may have been a few months during my own
infancy when the concept of motherhood was beyond my grasp,
but those days are dark to a memory of anything. One of my very
first recollections is of watching my newborn cousin sucking
happily at his mother's breast. I hovered close, spellbound, not
wanting to miss one detail, every sense awakening. His smell, his
noises, his breathing left their imprint on me. *I want a baby like
that* was a conscious thought as I observed the change of
mustardy diapers that followed. From that day, it was no longer
a matter of choice; it was simply a matter of time. It wasn't the
sight of my unveiled auntie or my exposed male cousin, though
both were remarkable enough. It was more than that. It was the
miracle, the wonder of it all. I was four. That afternoon the
decision was made.

Being born in 1947, into a tiny, white-fenced East York bungalow, had a great deal to do with my early resolution. At a time when girls could expect to become mothers or teachers or nurses, this was an unremarkable choice. But then, the optimistic Fifties and the thoughtful Sixties came along and with them the notion of broader choices, of *real* destinies, was held out to the female psyche. I never once waved a yellow chrysanthemum from a burlap-draped arm to prove my loyalty to Flower Power. Nor in the Seventies was I ever demonstrative enough to march for Women's Lib. But I was there, observing (a lifelong practice for me), silently rooting, hoping with all my heart that the world held equality and opportunity for all. We needed only to believe and love each other enough; the rest would look after itself.

Long before hippies and Joan Baez, my parents had somehow transmitted to their two daughters the idea that girls could be something other than teachers and nurses, not that there was anything wrong with either, if it was a vocation. My sister and I were never told, however subtly, that there were things we couldn't do or be. We were brought up to think for ourselves, do our best, experiment — as long as the experiments were legal. We were encouraged to read, to make things, to question, to try.

When I was eight, my parents bought a bigger home in Leaside, but for a long time, even though I had acquired my own bedroom, I missed our old house on Fairside Avenue. Shy and reluctant to make new friends, I began to hone my maternal instincts on an unwilling assortment of sick and wounded animals. Stunned birds usually died, but were treated to dignified funerals. Only a bat, declared rabid by my mother, was given the boot; the rest of the menagerie was allowed to stay long enough to recover. When I began luring the neighbourhood cats into the garage in the full belief — or at least hope — that they were strays, my parents bought us a kitten to go with Lucky, our sleepy old cocker spaniel. I began collecting different species of spiders in jars. They were tolerated, I suspect, because they kept mother's fervently disliked sister-in-law at bay. She refused to enter the house as long as my collection was intact, so the collection flourished. Live-bearing tropical fish survived fin rot and ich and brought forth in the basement. Snails hummed with their dual sexuality, and, despite the cat's ability to scoop a fair-sized harvest every night, the subterranean population grew under my supervision.

In the kitchen, Popeye the budgie hung over the sink, the only place safe from Twink, the cat. For seven years Popeye threw seed husks and the clips from his cuttlebone treats into my mother's hair as she worked at the sink. It's a good thing "he" turned out to be a mute "she"; had Popeye ever mimicked anything, it would have been a string of obscenities. In the yard I kept a tank filled with tadpoles, all of which developed admirable legs. Two small turtles didn't last as long as the tortoise, Virginia Woolf, who for the most part lived in a carton, but often turned up under the radiator.

Mitzi, a small Yorkshire terrier purchased when Lucky died at seventeen, was my best friend. She reigned on all floors and spent untold hours dutifully learning every trick I could devise. Her *pièce de résistance* was her ability to speak — really speak. I taught her to call me "Mama" by getting her to growl and to roll her tongue effectively. After she mastered that, she managed a remarkably clear "I Want One" for those times when anyone was eating potato chips or peanuts. I thought I was on a roll and tried in vain to teach her to hum, but Mitzi had no musical aptitude and people simply took her for hostile when she trotted past them growling in her gravelly monotone. Mitzi was a hit with most of our friends, except for one who accused my father of throwing his voice and another who fled the house, believing he had drunk too much.

The most exciting — and instructive — experiments were

always carried out in my sister Carolyn's room. Being four and a
half years younger, I could be persuaded to be her willing volunteer, until the night she almost blinded me by making me stare
for thirty minutes at a candle flame placed exactly ten inches
from my nose in a darkened room. When I began to whine and
droop, she turned on the light and reread the instructions. Thirty
minutes was in reality supposed to be thirty seconds, so we never
found out whether or not I was a good subject for hypnosis.
Blindness was a more immediate concern.

We thought our ventures in photography were successful, but
they were cut short by our indignant and humiliated father. We
had tried what we thought would be discreetly lit silhouettes of
each other. To achieve the desired effect we had gone topless,
which in my case made no difference and worked artistically. But
Carolyn, at thirteen, was endowed with a more-than-pert adoles-
cent figure, and apparently my camera had an acute parallax
problem. Our dad, who was then the city editor at the *Toronto
Telegram*, took our roll of film in to be developed by his colleagues in the darkroom. He was not pleased when an embarrassed photographer delivered the prints to him personally. After
a long discussion on pornography versus art, we had a clearer
idea of why he was so upset. We were allowed to keep our cameras, and, for him, we swore to keep our clothes on and our silhouettes in check forevermore.

Carolyn preferred goldfish to my tropical ones. I did too, in
terms of aesthetics. But good looks didn't hold a candle to all the
babies I could produce with my fertile pair of black mollies. But
soon the scientific challenge of actually aiding procreation fell
upon us, and we decided to breed her egg layers. The whole
thing had gone without a hitch. We had squeezed fat, fertile
Miriam of her eggs, milked the nameless-but-cooperative male,
and stirred the brew fastidiously. We thought the eggs were well
and truly done. It's hard to tell with fish eggs, but our book

encouraged us to believe that life was present. We kept them in a shallow bowl on top of the bedroom lamp, where they would be warm and safe from their cannibalistic parents. Day after day we watched and replenished the water as it evaporated. Gradually little dark spots, which grew ever larger and turned out to be eyes, developed. My rapture was almost complete when movement was detected and Carolyn told me I could have some of the babies for my part in the hatching. Then disaster struck. One day, neither of us checked the water. I stared down at forty-some-odd fried fish eyes and wept, bereft. The experiment was over, but the lesson wasn't. Being a mother, even to eggs, carried awesome responsibility, incredible heartache, and no small amount of guilt.

While all this was happening, I took particular delight in drawing. The long hours I spent doing it gave me time to ponder and analyze everything going on around me. By age ten, I had begun to paint in oils. Muddy copies of Christmas cards, kittens from the front page of the *Star Weekly*, any images that caught my eye and my fancy began to appear and were hung proudly all over the living room walls. My older sister emerged from her incense-filled bedroom, where she performed Japanese tea ceremonies and read haiku, long enough to be infected by the smell of turpentine and linseed oil. My parents, sensing talent and pleased that their daughters showed signs of not following the crowd, turned over the garage. It was emptied, an old carpet was laid, and paints, easels, and canvas were provided. So what if the car was rusting at the bottom of the drive? We had a studio.

Carolyn, now fifteen, produced lurid copies of her favourite, Henri Rousseau, while my projects expanded in size. My first commission came from an appreciative and indulgent friend of the family. For him I produced a mural of immense proportion, a history of civilization told through the development of art and architecture. It was a spectacle, rendered for the most part in a variety of poison greens, but in its creation that summer I taught myself to stretch canvas, to glaze, to scumble, and to paint with a palette knife.

Neighbours frequently arrived to peer through the doorway or actually join in the daily 3 p.m. tea ceremony that had been relocated to the garage. Pithy haikus were still read with great restraint as befitted the form, but now a dash of Leonard Cohen was added for variety's sake. Carolyn had taken to wearing lacquered chopsticks in her hair. I never had hair thick enough to support such touches, so I thoughtfully chewed my paintbrush ends during these breaks from my green opus and watched for reactions. "Oh," was usually the only comment made in our presence, but I'm certain tongues wagged elsewhere. My parents seemed amused that despite our Waspish surroundings we did not conform to the neighbourhood norm. By now, the idea of being different was becoming a source of delight rather than pain, even to Carolyn and me.

Proof that I had listened to my parents and betrayed the guidance counsellor at Leaside High came when I enrolled at the Ontario College of Art and entertained dreams of becoming the greatest Canadian painter of all time. Later, when I came to see that becoming immortal through talent required exceptional ability and slavish dedication, the urge to be someone's mother was strengthened, and artistic aspirations abandoned. Procreation, after all, is our answer to immortality. The motherhood urge had been planted and nurtured. It was probably traceable all the way back to some Neanderthal female who had painted cave walls as she suckled twin offspring. That first look at my baby cousin had simply triggered some time-dimmed genetic memory.

So I strummed my guitar and kept my brassiere firmly in place while other young women burned their underwear and wasted untold amounts of energy telling a bemused and uncaring world who they were. I worked at being a good designer and a passable artist. They raged with the magnificent fire of radical youth in possession of a just cause. They became disillusioned. I did, too, but even so, gains were made. We all got jobs, some got married, many got divorced, everybody grew older and, sadly, much more ordinary.

I never consciously decided against marriage, but even though playing the field had its moments, my Prince Charming never made himself known. Friends told me my expectations were too high. Maybe, but lowering them at that point seemed silly. I simply never understood the pressure to "find a man" the way they did. After they were settled with their choices, I became the focus of another crusade. The "Get-Kath-Hooked-Up" campaign lasted quite a few years. I didn't enjoy or understand their need to partner me with a string of blind dates and "wonderful guys." Most of them revealed themselves as sex-starved creeps or crashing bores within the first five minutes of a liaison. A golf pro, who was described as "misunderstood and disillusioned by aggressive women," arrived at my door and asked if we would be sharing my bed or his; if it was to be mine, he would bring his things in from the car right away. I should never have gone with him to The Inn on the Park where a pianist friend of his was playing. After he introduced me as "The Broad" I was finally offended enough to take a washroom break and a taxi home. The only good thing about the evening was that his things were still in his car. That saved me from having to answer the door when he stood pounding on it and yelling unpleasant things a half hour later.

Then there was his polar opposite, the brilliant brother of a friend's husband. Definitely Ivy League, with "a future in banking." No damned wonder. He would walk me blocks in the pouring rain, oblivious to running makeup and dissolving hair spray, in order to take advantage of some cheap hourly parking rate. His idea of a stimulating evening was to sit at my place calculating how many pounds per square inch of water pressure were exerted on the glass sides of my forty-gallon octagonal aquarium. I didn't care, and the fish didn't either, so he went the way of the others. This much fun I could have by myself.

There were very nice men in between, but not one ever kissed me on the eyelids or begged me to go horseback riding on a white sand beach — my idea of exquisite romance. Too many dinners ended in fiasco, as we were serenaded by paid musicians trying to create ambience and put us in the mood. This seemed artificial and for some mysterious reason never failed to render me utterly hysterical, no matter how hard I fought to look lovesick. The confused faces of suitors always made it worse, and I spent many evenings being sorry and trying to explain myself.

It came, then, as an immense relief when my friends gave up and I was allowed to relax and let things flow in a more natural, spontaneous way. The fact that nothing really happened after that was, by this time, of no concern to me. I was content in knowing I would have my baby and my career — with or without a man. The "how" was becoming clearer. I made up my mind to adopt a child if, by thirty, I hadn't found my life partner. I don't know why, maybe too many fish had taken the excitement out of it, but it wasn't important to me to make a baby; it was simply imperative to have one. It was all quite simple. I was woman, I was invincible, and by twenty-nine, I was ready.

3

IT WAS BEST NOT TO MENTION NAKED COUSINS OR TROPICAL FISH

The desire to begin formal adoption proceedings was growing into an obsession as I neared thirty. My career was looking good and I had been at it long enough to feel secure. I enjoyed being the art director of Scholastic, a major children's book publisher, even with its moments of tension and pressure. I was making more money than one person needed. It was time to turn intentions into action.

I had had many discussions with my mother and sister about my approaching birthday and the self-imposed time limit connected to it. Both understood, and my mother wasn't in any position to question the notion of adoption or how I had come by it in the first place. She and my father had adopted a seven-month-old baby boy when Carolyn and I were twenty-five and twenty-one. The whole procedure from start-up to placement had taken five months. Mom and Dad were somewhere in their mid-fifties and considered very radical, if not mad, by many of our friends and relatives. To the amazement of most of them, the whole thing was going marvellously. My parents had never been happier, and Jason was a thriving, beautiful boy. He was also thoroughly nice.

There were rumours, naturally, that Jason was really mine, fathered while I was away visiting my sister, who was by that time married and living in Jamaica. The fact that I never stayed away longer than ten days and carried the child with nary a bulge didn't seem to matter. I would have been proud to admit Jason was my son, if he had been. In fact, I wished he was. I was still living at home when he arrived and I loved him with a passion. When he was three, I moved to my own apartment because I felt it would be confusing and unfair to all of us if I didn't fade back to the status of sister. My parents were his parents, and I had to come to terms with that. I was clever enough to see that the move was best, but I was attached enough to stay very close to the homestead. My new apartment was within walking distance and Jason travelled back and forth with me at regular intervals for babysitting, visits, and play.

Carolyn's son, Chris, and my brother were only six months apart in age, which seemed to baffle everyone: that and the fact that they both shared black/white heritage. My nephew and brother were roughly the same size and shade, but there the similarity ended. Nevertheless, strangers always took them for brothers and often as twins. If confusion reigned around us, we had no difficulty with it, even when Carolyn and Chris arrived back in Canada to stay. Having two little boys around the place only made everything nicer. Chris and Jason had each other and were close friends. The boys were eight when I began actively promoting the idea that I was ready to begin my own family.

Even with Carolyn and Mom onside, I was a little nervous about how my father would react to my plan. I knew he would eventually come around, but I did think he would resist at the outset and find all sorts of sensible reasons why, in my case, this wasn't a good idea. I didn't relish the thought of having to battle my father into understanding. But whether it was because my mother had already paved the way, or whether I had misjudged him, I needn't have worried. Coward that I was, I waited until he was sick with the flu before broaching the subject. In his weakened state he weighed everything I told him carefully and then accepted the news like a lamb.

"I guess you know what you're doing," he said. "Your mother and I will help any way we can for as long as you need us."

I accepted his promise that night and have made use of it many times, perhaps many times more than he intended.

◄◦►

It was 1975 and the world was a troubled place. Vietnam was constantly in the news. Reports were confusing and coloured by Western bias, but one thing was clear: the situation was deteriorating and coming to a close. And it was creating orphans — planeloads of them. Emergency airlifts of children were being hastily planned, and as I read about them, I was certain that my little one must be among those coming to homes in Canada. The Sixties had made their mark on me. I had a social conscience and, moreover, I didn't have any particular desire to see my own traits handed on to some other poor soul. Flat feet, a weak spine and a double chin are nothing to hold out for. It would be easy to love a child who didn't look like me. I wanted to give an existing child with no parents one good one, rather than setting out to place yet another baby on an already-strained planet.

The realization that it was time to stop talking and get on with it came as an intimidating thrill. I was breathless and my hands shook as I spoke on the telephone to Helen Allen, a family friend and a past employee of my father's old newspaper, the *Toronto Telegram*. Her column, "Today's Child," had run for years and had been picked up by the *Toronto Star* when the *Telegram* folded.

My parents had turned to her for guidance on how to begin Jason's adoption. She had taken an active interest in Jason, as she did with many of the children placed through her column, and complained loudly if her Christmas card didn't contain the mandatory photo every year. If Helen was surprised to hear from me, her voice didn't betray it. She did tell me adopting would be more difficult now than it had been for Mom and Dad because there were fewer children available for placement. She also warned that being single wouldn't make things easier. Having said that, she didn't hesitate to tell me who to get in touch with.

I called the Children's Aid Society as soon as its offices opened the next morning. The intake worker asked a few basic questions and arranged for me to come a week later for an interview. It was all in a day's work for her, and after pencilling me into her schedule, she probably never gave that first call another thought. For me, on the other hand, it was the starter's pistol; I was finally off and running. I spent the better part of the week anticipating each question, mulling over every possible response, and running to the bathroom — the result of a nervous stomach.

In those days I was quite thin and I suspect I really didn't look all that bad as I headed down to Charles Street on a glorious, sunny September morning. I had spent the weekend finding the perfect new outfit and shoes and was genuinely pleased with the results. The shoes were even comfortable.

I had long legs and once I was sitting down, I could sometimes manage to look elegant and cool if I crossed them just the right way. I tried this, in an effort to quell the cramps and to keep the Children's Aid woman from noticing the ashen pallor of my skin. I waited for the questioning to begin. I had no intention of misrepresenting anything, but I couldn't help thinking that the course of my future, and someone else's, depended on how this pleasant, white-haired woman reacted to whatever I might say in the next thirty minutes.

My mind was a total blank as I graced her with what I hoped was a confident, pleasant smile. How she began is a blur, but I remember being aware of gentle probes here and there into my personal life, my sexual orientation, my financial stability, and my overall sanity. I knew the questions were all in the interest of the child, my child, so I wasn't the least bit upset with the path we followed. Still, nothing of what I rehearsed all week remained in my brain or exited my mouth. I was flying blind and imagining I was doing pretty well until she asked why I wanted a baby at all. It didn't take a psychic to sense it was best not to mention naked cousins or tropical fish at this point. I stalled for a moment, then gave it my best shot.

"Haven't you ever visited friends who have just had a baby?" I asked.

"Of course."

"Did you ask them why they wanted it?"

"No."

"Me either. I took it for granted they had made a decision and were happy with the outcome. I have always wanted a child and I've thought a great deal about it. Not only that, but there are kids already born who could use a good mother. I know I'd be an improvement over lots of couples who never had to apply to have a baby."

The woman settled back in her chair and nodded her under-standing. She fiddled with a pen for a moment and then put another question to me. "But what if, after you have the child, you meet someone you want to marry or have children with?"

The question seemed to imply shallow intent on my part. I tried not to sound testy, but probably failed. "It's not that I'm looking for a child to fill my time with until something better comes along. I'm not a kid anymore. I can't imagine falling in love with someone who wouldn't accept the fact that I've had a life before him. By my age lots of people have been in and out of marriages already. Some of them have children, and their lives aren't over. At least I'm coming at single parenthood by choice, not by accident or through loss. If somebody else can't accept that and love my child along with me, then he's not who I want to marry."

The woman jotted down a few notes before looking up to scrutinize my face one more time. "And you would be prepared to live with that?" Her voice had dropped to a whisper and sounded sympathetic.

I softened a little. "It might not make me happy, but it would be pretty clear cut. I'm sorry. I don't know what makes me want a child, I just do. Judging from the number of strollers on the street, it doesn't seem all that unnatural."

The woman across from me smiled. I decided to state my position clearly, one last time.

"Look," I said, "I'm not prepared to sit around forever waiting for someone who may or may not exist. I've had a long go and a good time being unattached, but now it's not enough. I'm going to have a baby one way or another, and this seems like the most responsible way to do it."

Embarrassed, I could feel my ears burning. I stared into my lap as silence surrounded us. Finally the woman dropped her pen and folded her hands. "Good," she said, smiling again, and I knew that she had finally heard whatever it was she had been probing for.

In return, I was given cautious encouragement, some papers to fill out, and the promise of a second interview. The next appointment would be with someone new, a case worker who would get to know me better, guide me through a maze of paper-work, do a home study, and become a face, a name, a friend I would never forget. I would never meet this first woman again. All I remember about her was how she looked inside me with X-ray vision — and that she was willing to push the rules just a little because of something she saw there.

I left the building knowing the first and most important test had been passed. Papers in hand, I skipped down the front steps, feeling good for the first time in days. My intestines felt like they had been unscrambled and soothed. Struggling to remind myself that time and patience would be necessary, I glowed with inner certainty. I was going to have my baby; there was no stopping me now.

If I had known then how complicated it would be, I probably would have calmed down considerably. I doubt that I would have given up on parenthood, but the concept of adoption might have been discarded in favour of Plan B: the abandonment of ideals and the production of someone with flat feet and a weak chin. But ignorance is bliss, so I set out on my journey to the Land of Motherhood, trembling with anticipation and determined to stick it out to a successful end, even if it killed me. Waiting twenty-nine years for just the right moment can do that to a person.

4

THIS, AFTER ALL,
WASN'T A BABY STORE

"You have to understand that this process could take two to three years. Things are different from when your parents adopted."

Three years. Sandra Scarth, my new case worker, looked directly into my face as I tried to hide any trace of disappointment. It wasn't too difficult. For one thing, I didn't fully believe her; I assumed she was painting the worst-case scenario in the event we hit snags along the way. Surely we would manage this in much less time. My parents had their son within five months of their initial interview and even if things had changed, it couldn't be by that much. Besides, if Sandra was bothering to caution me, she was definitely considering going all the way and I was too elated to fully relate to what she was saying. "It's all right," I told her. "You don't know how long I've already waited. Three years is nothing compared to that."

Sandra smiled evenly and relaxed a little behind her well-worn desk. The room we were in was a giant step down from the administrative office I had visited earlier. This low, shaded building on Huntley Street in midtown Toronto was nearby, but it was older, busier, and in much more need of a good paint job. Clearly, this was where the day-to-day business of the Toronto East Branch of the Children's Aid Society was carried out and from my brief wait in the reception area, I knew that adoption was not the only family issue dealt with here.

We had talked for more than an hour and it was almost time to go. Sandra reached into her drawer and pulled out a sheaf of papers. "We require you to have three unrelated references, preferably married couples. I recommend that at least one couple be your own age. They should fill in these forms, understanding that what they say is in confidence. Once they have been completed, they should be returned directly to me. These forms are for you, and we need this filled in by your employer. Then there's the personal essay. I always think that's the hardest part, but we find it very useful. It's good if you can include some personal photos as well." Sandra had handed me each paper as she spoke. "There's something else you should know. When a couple comes here, I, along with my supervisor, can decide if we'll go ahead. When single applicants come, the decision has to be made by a larger group. Once your papers are all back to us, we will have to meet and review the case before I can complete a home study."

A slight feeling of nervousness was pushed aside by my affection for this new person in my life. She was tall, slim, about thirty-five, and very attractive. Sandra had a way of putting me at ease immediately upon my arrival and though she delved and probed, her questions were delivered with just the right mix of familiarity and professionalism. From the start I had the impression she was an ally and someone who, once committed, would be almost as dogged as I.

I had come to the meeting determined not to have too many demands about the child I wanted. This, after all, wasn't a baby store. But I had to admit that when we first saw Jason, the fact that he was a beautiful, bright, healthy child brought immense joy and relief — the same, I suppose, as any parents feel when they see their "perfect" infant for the first time.

I hadn't been with Sandra long before I felt confident enough to admit that I did have a basic idea of the child I wanted. I longed for a little girl, for one thing. I thought it would be easier for me to raise a girl alone than a boy, though the data I had to base that opinion on was limited. I was pleased when the social worker told me there was a policy to match the sex of the child with that of the applicant in single-parent adoptions. At least my first request hadn't upset the applecart. Braver, I went on to add that I hoped the child would be healthy and bright enough to take advantage of an education. Finally, I expressed the hope that my little girl would be as young as possible, without saying just how young I hoped that would be. Thanks to endless hours of babysitting I had put in as a teenager, as well as having my infant brother arrive when I was twenty-one, I was thoroughly at ease handling small babies.

So much can be given or denied to any child in the early months and that made me anxious. All my life I had watched women smiling into the faces of their tiny infants, echoing baby noises, touching, nodding encouragement at each fragile attempt to try something new. I wanted to be the one to bestow high praise when finally brain, muscle, and desire worked together, and a tiny hand reached for and grasped the thing it was seeking. I wanted to relish and be part of every major milestone: first smile, first tooth, first steps, first words.

Of course, my requests were similar to everyone else's and now I was on weak ground. Sandra had repeatedly mentioned all those childless couples who wanted perfect newborns. Immediately I felt both selfish and unjustly denied. I had some nerve, turning up here without a husband and asking for the same thing as everybody else. But since I was here, damn it, why should I be the one to deny that my own wishes were as valid as theirs? On the other hand, if I stressed the point too much, I could be making Sandra's task impossible. Concessions made me nervous and I was scared even as I made mine. I allowed as to how I would consider a little girl up to age four, but I sincerely hoped she would be much younger than that. Just as pregnancy carries so many risks, so does adoption. In both instances a myriad of things can go wrong before the baby is even born. But afterwards, in the case of adoption, for however long it takes, you must rely on how well a number of total strangers played their part in nurturing your child and bringing your family to you. It wasn't a comforting thought.

The interview had gone well, and I was relieved when Sandra stood and reached out to shake my hand. "I'll give you lots of time to fill in your papers and let you know when the three reference forms have been returned to me. I expect we can set up another appointment in a month or two."

"A month! Can't it be sooner? I'm sure I can have these done by next week."

Sandra laughed. "Two to three years, remember? There's no panic with the paperwork."

At this rate I could easily see how so much time could pass. But as of today the clock was running and the game was to see how much time we could shave off the record. "What if we set a date for the end of next week and cancel if we're not ready?" I asked.

Sandra had practice with the likes of me. She shook her head and chuckled. "All right. I'll put you down for next week, same time."

I was already beginning to sift through names as I walked through the parking lot to the car. My best friend from college was married now, and had just had a baby. I was certain Margaret and her husband, Bob, would understand and agree to write a reference. Good. That was the married couple my own age. The next choice was easy. I had boarded with neighbours across from my parents' house when Dad had taken a post in New York as a United Nations bureau chief during my second year of college. They had known me since I was ten, but that one year certainly cemented our relationship. Jean and Vern were educational consultants and highly regarded in the field. The third references would be Cathy and Shaun. We had known them since their arrival in Canada, and they were staunch family people with three children and strong ties to their church and community. They had taken special delight in Jason's arrival and were among the friends who had supported my parents' decision 100 percent. They would understand mine, I was sure. By the time I pulled into my parents' drive, the list was complete.

Later that evening, when I was discussing my choices with Mom, I was unaware that Jason was listening from the living room. After I left he went to our mother and asked why I hadn't chosen him. He would have written a reference and felt very hurt not to be picked. While I was busy recruiting help, he was busy composing his recommendation. The next day he stood beaming proudly beside me as I read his letter. But his eager face crumpled when, unexpectedly, I started to cry. I reached for him, but Jason fled to the basement, upset at my tears. I found him sitting in an old chair in the corner.

"Jase," I said. "That was the nicest letter anyone could write."

"But it made you cry," he said, fidgeting with his fingers and close to tears himself.

"Don't you know people sometimes cry when they're very happy?"

The poor child shook his head. "Well, they do," I continued. "And you make me happier than anyone I know."

"Happy enough to make you cry?" he asked, beginning to look pleased.

"Yep," I told him, giving him a hug. "But try not to do it too often, OK? It's hard work, being that happy."

My brother grinned. "I hope you get your baby, Kath."

"I hope so, too. But whether I do or not, you know I'll always love you, don't you?"

Jason nodded but now his eyes were shiny. "Wait a minute," I said. "Are those tears for happy or for sad?"

"Happy — mostly," he answered.

"Well, make sure they are, because no little baby is going to take your place with me." We emerged from the basement, equilibrium restored. I pocketed the letter and took it home, intending to keep it.

I had some work of my own to do. The form for my employer was simple enough, verifying my good work habits, length of employment, and salary. The hard part was bringing the subject up at all with my very nice, but very traditional, managing director. I even wore a new dress for the occasion, but I should have paid more for it. As I sat in his office perspiring madly and trying to explain my situation, the dye began to run. At the end of the meeting I sauntered coolly out the door — and headed straight for the washroom to mop up, my armpits an alarming shade of dark olive green. The pattern of yellow and black elephants, so perky scant moments before, was a blurred mess from the brassiere line up, and I spent the rest of the day with my arms pinned tightly to my sides. The dress, regretfully, had to go in the trash, but it had served its purpose. Fortunately my underarms returned to their normal shade in due time.

I needn't have been so nervous. Either my boss figured I was a hopeless case, or he gathered I knew what I was doing. He uttered all the encouraging and hopeful sounds he was capable of and I had my signed papers in hand by the end of the day. His secretary brought them with a little smile in an envelope marked "PERSONAL." To my surprise there was a very nicely worded letter attached to the forms: an added endorsement and a lovely gesture on his part.

Sandra had been quite correct. The personal essay was difficult. I was supposed to describe myself, my motivations, my qualifications, my dreams for this child, and the family I was setting out to form. I found enough photos to give a pretty good idea of me, my home, and surroundings. But the written part felt like a trap. It's far easier to ask someone else to say things about you than to do it yourself. Should I admit I was shy, insecure, scared, an athletic klutz who intended to introduce my child to everything except sports — especially ice skating? Should I own up to being competent, diligent, determined, somewhat talented? Should I be modest and risk underselling? Should I brag and risk overkill? I started and restarted the thing until, beaten by fatigue, I convinced myself I had a good mix of everything. Ironically, I was the one who came closest to causing a postponement of my appointment due to lack of paperwork.

I did just make it back to Sandra's office the following week, forms complete and all references accounted for. She told me that the people I had chosen had all responded with remarkable comments in my favour and she had been very impressed with the quality and thought put into them. At that point I decided to give her Jason's letter.

"My brother wrote this," I said, fumbling in my purse. "I know it's not what you're looking for because he is related and definitely not a married couple. But he is adopted and he knows me well. Maybe you won't think it counts, but he wanted to recommend me." Sandra took the scrap of paper from me and read Jason's letter:

I think that my sister Kathie would be a very good mother for a baby girl. She lives in a nice place and when she is at work I will help look after her baby, because I was adopted too and she helped look after me. She would be a good mother because she is nice and fun. She loves children quite a lot I know because she has been my sister for 8 years and we love each other.

Jason Cole

"I think it counts," Sandra said quietly. "I'd like to include this when I present your case at our next review. It's the most eloquent reference you could have asked for."

I left the battle-worn building on Huntley Street with a feeling of absolute certainty. Sandra was behind me, the papers were complete and deemed to be well done. The panel would accept my application and allow Sandra to finish a home study.

There were indeed more visits and many more talks. Sandra would come to my apartment twice and add its description to her report. Eventually, having exhausted the subject of family and child rearing, we would discuss movies, literature, careers, ballet — whatever flowed between two people who liked each other well enough to climb uphill together for three years, or longer if necessary, in order to perform a miracle.

5

"THE PRICE OF INSURANCE
HAS RISEN SLIGHTLY"

Five months passed, the length of time it had taken for Jason's placement. I was nowhere near completion of my mission, but I couldn't pretend I hadn't been warned. There was still no great alarm when a year and then eighteen months had passed. With each week, I felt both closer to, and farther from, success.

Each raise and promotion was duly reported to the Children's Aid, making my position stronger, but not furthering the cause in any way. By now I was running an art department of six. Ultimately, I was responsible for the look of a burgeoning Canadian publishing program — all the books, catalogues, and promotional material to leave the building. Still, I had no one to spend my paycheque on but myself.

Communication with Sandra Scarth by now was initiated mostly by me. I would call occasionally to chat, but really to remind her I was still there and still waiting. Sandra was always fairly optimistic, but had less and less to tell me. Now and then she would send an article on studies of single-parent adoptions or some such thing to keep me posted. Sometimes she requested documentation on salary increases and medical exams. Shortly after our third anniversary passed, she called me at work. She sounded serious. Immediately I knew something was up.

"I'm becoming increasingly concerned. There are fewer and fewer children available these days for placement and more and more couples piling up on the waiting list. Some of the social workers do not believe in single-parent adoptions. You are facing biases I cannot easily overcome."

"But —"

"I know *you* would accept a child of mixed race, but there's escalating pressure from outside as well as within the Society to place those children with minority families. There may be children available in other provinces, or overseas, but I can't devote the necessary time exploring these options. I promise to keep trying, but I really think you should start acting on your own behalf outside the country."

I felt cut adrift. "But how do I contact people outside Canada?"

"I can put you in touch with Derek White at the federal government's International Adoption Desk and send him copies of your papers. There are agencies he might be able to connect you with."

I didn't know how to protest or what to say. Sandra worked to fill the silence. "I will supply you with your home study in case you come up with leads of your own, and I'll back you with all I can. I'm sorry, but I really think it's your best bet."

I couldn't believe this. After three years of hoping, waiting, and planning, I was still at the starting line. I had been standing there while every pair before and after my entry to the race passed by. I felt angry and betrayed. Sandra knew what was going through my mind.

"It's not the end of the road," she said. "It's just another way to look into things, another way to start. I promise I'll still be working from this end."

◄○►

The good thing about not knowing where to start is that you can jump in almost anywhere. And at least now I could take an active part in my own fate. Whatever failure or success was to come, it would be of my own making.

I made copies of my home study and began a campaign involving the mental resources of my entire family. First attempts were random and ill-conceived, but we gained practice as we went along.

At the time, Carolyn was working at the *Toronto Sun*. The newspaper was full of the horrendous human tragedy that had overtaken part of a nation. One of the paper's reporters was leaving for Hong Kong to do a story on the refugees — tagged as The Boat People — who were arriving in that harbour in droves. A flurry of letter writing and photocopying produced a package for him to carry along and he was decent enough to oblige. Two weeks later he was back and my envelope was plopped on Carolyn's desk with a brief note explaining the situation.

> *Carolyn,*
> *Sorry. I didn't find one orphan, as I tried to explain in one story. Nevertheless, the Hong Kong immigration officer knows about your sister and will call me if anything is possible.*

Hong Kong was an avenue I explored myself to no avail when I was there on business a few months later, checking the colour quality of five picture books scheduled for fall.

In the meantime, my father suggested I call his friend William

Newell, executive director of World Vision. William was only too happy to write a friend of his in South Korea on my behalf. Within a few weeks, I was communicating directly with authorities there and to my surprise things were going well. I almost stopped breathing the day a letter arrived with a photo of a little girl named Kim Chee who was two years old. Along with the picture came instructions to apply to immigration and send more documentation and more letters from my doctor, bank, and employer. It was all done and notarized in a flash.

Then, with equal speed, a curtain was lowered. Any hope that Kim Chee would be mine disappeared when President Park of South Korea was assassinated. From that point on, no letters were answered; no news ever came. After a long silence I had to face the truth. The little girl in the orange dress who stood in stocking feet at the foot of a staircase would never come to Canada. Much later, I was updated by Employment and Immigration Canada.

> *Dear Client:*
>
> *This refers to your sponsorship application on behalf of Kim Chee Jung. We have just been advised by the Canadian Embassy in Hong Kong that the Korean government does not allow a single parent to adopt children.*
>
> *Regretfully, under these circumstances we have no alternative but to close our file.*
>
> *Yours very truly.*

I already knew hope was gone, but even so, as I held her photograph I wept long and hard for the loss of Kim Chee. Eventually, I placed the picture back in its envelope and wrapped it in tissue paper, along with a little dress I had made. I hid them both away on a shelf in my clothes closet.

The Children's Aid, meanwhile, contacted the International

Adoption Desk in Ottawa. Shortly afterwards I was advised to write to a woman named Sandra Simpson. She wasn't altogether unknown to me, as her face had been appearing frequently in the press and on television. She had a large adopted family of her own and ran an agency called Families For Children. The agency was responsible for bringing many children to homes in Canada. Apparently, Sandra Simpson had no difficulty accepting single applicants, but she did advise that I would have to be willing to take an older child or one with a disability or questionable health.

While I was establishing contact with Sandra Simpson and dealing with yet another set of applications and requirements, another possibility presented itself. One of our neighbours, a young woman in her early twenties, had gone to Calcutta to work as a volunteer for Mother Theresa. She had done a stint in the hospital for the terminally ill, but was now working in an orphanage. I wrote to her and was rewarded with her usual optimistic response to a challenge. Alex was delighted by my decision and would do everything she could to help. She was, after all, at "the source."

We wrote many letters over the months that followed as Alex pursued leads for me there. Then one day I received Alex's letter with information and forms from a woman who ran an agency specializing in international adoptions. Once again, papers were filled out and mailed, and for a while excitement ran high, despite warnings from my friends at the Children's Aid to be wary; they had not heard of this agency or this Mrs. Singh. Still, with Alex there to look after my interests, they had to admit it was worth looking into. Then, to my delight, Mrs. Singh wrote to say she was coming to Canada for a visit and would make time to see me.

I telephoned Burlington, home of another organization, the Kuan Yin Society, which had brought children to homes in

Canada. According to her letter, Mrs. Singh had an appointment with them. But when I asked about the woman's credentials, I was told that though they had heard of her, they had not agreed to see her. In fact, if she was coming, she would not be allowed through the doors. Shaken a bit, I called Helen Allen. She had never heard of the woman either and was dubious. With Helen's words of caution still fresh in my ears, I decided to drive to Burlington and have lunch with Mrs. Singh. I would try to make up my own mind after that.

Mrs. Singh stated a preference for Italian food and we found a fashionable restaurant where we could talk. Somewhere between salad and dessert, I became uneasy. This little lady, so sweetly benign at first, began to ask too many questions that went well beyond what anyone else had wanted to know. All of them had to do with my income and contacts. Not one of them was about me or the kind of person I was. She obviously expected me to pay for lunch and I happily did. At her suggestion I walked with her through some nearby shops. After many sighs and comments as to the price of various items, it became very clear she was asking me to purchase things for her to take home as gifts. I didn't take the broad hint on the shopping, even when she coyly said how much her daughter would love a certain very expensive Italian ceramic bowl. Then, ever so easily, she stated that if I should want a healthy baby, I would have to be willing to pay "insurance money." Her problem, she said, was that she was always spending so much on saving little souls that her resources were spent. The atmosphere was becoming strained, but turned positively icy when I told her I didn't have the four-thousand-dollar insurance fee with me. She offered to take a cheque, but I told her I needed to consider everything she had said carefully.

The encounter ended moments later when she told me one final chilling story. The last woman she had placed a baby with had not cooperated fully. As a result, there had been no money to do a thorough check of the child's health. Unfortunately, after placement it was discovered that the little girl was blind. Such a tragedy, and so easily avoided — if only the woman had sent the insurance money. Advising me to call her if I should wish to pay for the child of my dreams, the woman turned and walked away without so much as a nod of farewell. The hem of her gold sari fluttered delicately as she padded away, leaving me, as she intended, forlorn and full of self-doubt.

I drove home, shaken and miserable. I didn't want to have anything more to do with this woman. Still, four thousand dollars wasn't much if it would deliver to me what I now ached for. The possibility that this woman might be buying or even kidnapping children was very real and very distressing. Even so, three years of getting nowhere had taken their toll. For the first time I was afraid — afraid of what this woman was doing and afraid it might be my only chance. If people were so despondent that they were willing to sell their own babies, surely the children were better off coming to homes like mine where they were wanted. Of course, I knew the issue wasn't that straightforward or clear-cut and suddenly I was angry. I had just eaten lunch with an unscrupulous individual who played on the emotions of desperate people on both sides of the world. She didn't care if mine was a good home or an abusive one. She didn't care if the child she sent was the right child for me. She didn't care if the parents she took it from were betrayed. She didn't care if children lived or died. She cared about being rich.

Tears rolled down my cheeks all the way home. By the time I reached the driveway, I had rejected temptation and the dark risks it carried. As compensation, I promised myself, I would get pregnant and have my own baby if all else failed. I never communicated with Mrs. Singh again, despite her two follow-up letters describing a newborn who could be made ready in time to be brought to Canada by Alex when she returned a few months later. Both letters ended with, "It is truly unfortunate that you hesitated on my original offer. Due to economic difficulties, the price of insurance has risen slightly . . . "

Eventually, Alex did come home, full of apologies and amazing stories, ending my on-the-spot contact. I would have to leave any prospects I might have in India to Sandra Simpson and her much-respected organization.

Then, one day out of the blue, Sandra Scarth phoned. "Kathryn? I have something I want you to consider. There's a baby in northern Ontario. She's only nine months old, very bright and beautiful. She has a minor handicap, but we don't expect it will slow her down much."

Sandra was excited and I listened as she went on to describe everything she knew about "Baby Laura." Both of her hands and feet were slightly malformed, but already she was showing signs of using them well. The authorities wanted her near a good paediatric hospital as well as the Hugh MacMillan Rehabilitation Centre, where they expected she could benefit greatly from surgery, physiotherapy, and counselling. I was extremely handy to both.

Initially, I had qualms about the deformities, but they didn't last long. Everything else about this little girl sounded wonderful and I began to think I could help her through any hardships and discomfort she might suffer. In fact, as a child I myself had worn leg braces and had managed to survive the taunts of being different. Maybe she and I would be a good match. Before the phone call ended, I was thoroughly excited.

But then the question of religion reared its ugly head. The baby's mother had stated that it would be nice if the adoptive home was Catholic, but that to her, the most important thing was a good, loving environment. However, when my home study arrived, her social worker placed much importance on my not being Catholic. Despite the fact that we lived twenty minutes from a world-renowned paediatric hospital and were within walking distance of the Hugh MacMillan Rehab Centre, and despite the knowledge that the baby's medical situation might work against her placement elsewhere, religion became the major issue. The social worker said she would find the baby a more suitable home. All I could do was hope that she did.

A month or so later, I faced an even more difficult situation. Families For Children called. They had a brother and sister they wanted kept together. The little girl was two and in fairly good health. Her five-year-old brother, however, was in poor condition. His tubercular spine was expected to kill him within the next year. If he survived at all, he would be badly crippled. There were no two ways about it; the children were to be adopted together. So there it was. I could have my daughter if I was willing to go through the heartache of losing my son. This called for much soul searching.

What kind of person would turn her back on these two children? How could I claim to have the qualities of a good parent if I wasn't willing to help them? Yet I couldn't deny the terror the whole idea instilled in me. My plan from the outset had been to adopt one child. Two children, even two healthy ones, would stretch my resources too far. This seemed foolhardy, to say the least. It wasn't a formula for happiness or even success. It was tailor-made for disaster. I doubted I would be able to remain philosophical about the little boy longer than thirty seconds after seeing him for the first time. He would creep into my heart and maintain a hold on it even after his death. Then what shape would I be in to raise his sister and blithely go on with life?

Everything about this whole process seemed unfair. Hadn't I told everyone quite openly what I thought I could handle right from the beginning? Surely couples would have twice the resources to deal with health and emotional problems or children who were older at the time of placement. I was angry and afraid to refuse, but it seemed wrong to change my plans after all this work and waiting. At least this time, there were no photos to haunt me. To my own shame and disappointment, I finally told them no. I would wait. As I hung up the phone, I was worried that my failure to rise to the occasion would hamper my prospects with Families For Children.

The battering of previous failed attempts was wearing me down. I was considering situations that I wouldn't have given a second thought to at the beginning. This was dangerous. Even so, I had just denied two very needy children entry to my home. They might never have a mother or a father. One of them might not even have the opportunity to die on clean sheets dampened with the tears of someone who would mourn his passing. I would never know if another chance came their way, and I would never have the courage to ask. I was selfish, but logic kept telling me I was crazy to contemplate this any longer. Still, if I couldn't accept what fate sent, what on earth was I doing tinkering with it at all?

For the first time I wondered if this whole thing had been a stupid, ill-conceived idea right from the start. The next couple of days I considered calling Sandra Scarth and telling her that I wanted to stop everything and give up. But I couldn't. Rather like someone who contemplates suicide but is prevented from it by the notion that the next day might be better, I hovered on the brink of quitting. But what if tomorrow I was contacted about a child that fit perfectly? I needed time to justify my stand, the same way a liar needs time to rationalize, lay blame elsewhere, and finally grant self-forgiveness. I took the time and made use of it. But like the liar, I knew something about myself now that I would have preferred to have hidden, even from me.

6

"WELL, WE DO HAVE ORPHANS . . . "

The March doldrums were in full swing and I was as down as anyone could get. My parents tried to convince me to go with them and Jason on a holiday to Barbados, but I was in no frame of mind to consider it. I had gone to my doctor and unloaded on her more than once. She had been supportive from the beginning and was still on the alert for a situation within her practice that might allow for a private adoption.

"The problem is, these days, not as many girls and women are having unwanted pregnancies," she said. "When I see a patient who is, I offer the alternative of abortion and it's often accepted. I'll keep you in mind, though, if I hear of anything."

Now I was asking her for names of hospitals that had artificial insemination clinics. The two available in Toronto at that time were of little use to me. After a phone call to each, I learned that only infertile couples were accepted to the programs. Single people didn't qualify. I found out about two American clinics that would comply. One was in Buffalo, the other in New York.

Knowing this was good enough for now. I could always resort to extreme measures, rather than come away from what by now was almost four years empty-handed. Still, something kept urging me to stick to my original game plan.

My parents pressed their invitation again. I was afraid I might miss a call from any one of the current leads I had going. I was waiting for news from four different countries, the Children's Aid Society, Families For Children, and my doctor, and hadn't been away from home more than once since the initial application had been submitted. I found myself not only reluctant to be away, but also unwilling to use vacation time. At that time, there was no such thing as adoption leave, so I kept hoarding my earned days off just in case. In the end it was the obsession itself that convinced me I needed a break and some physical distance from the subject. I realized I was tying myself down more just waiting for a child than if I already had one. Still, as I packed, I threw in copies of all my documents. I felt incomplete without them.

◄○►

Two days of lying on the beach and playing with my brother had a wonderful effect. I was feeling relaxed and happy for the first time in ages. On the third day, Dad rented a car and we took off for a discovery tour of the island.

The interior was surprisingly dry and after one too many cane fields, I was feeling drowsy in the back seat. As I drifted off, I glanced sideways and saw a low cement block building sliding out of sight. The building itself was unremarkable. The sign in front of it was not: ORPHANAGE.

"Stop the car," I said. "Let's go back and see what that was."

My long-suffering parents exchanged a look, but Dad turned the car around and stopped in front of the drive. "What do you think?" he asked. "Should we go in?"

Jason and I were all for it, but Mom was hesitant. "I guess so, but Kath, contain yourself in there. Don't go falling in love with the first child you see."

"I won't," I agreed, already climbing out of the backseat.

The interior of the building was spotless and airy despite the brilliant sun overhead. Ceiling fans and subdued lighting helped keep the place cool. At first there seemed to be no one in charge, and we walked farther down the hallway. Finally a large woman in a nurse's uniform came smiling towards us. "Yes?" she asked. "Is there something I can do for you?"

I told her my story and asked if she could help. The woman said I would have to go into the Welfare Services in Bridgetown and speak to the authorities there. "This is just where the children are sent to be cared for," she said. "I have no power to place any of them. I would be happy to show you around though, if you like."

We followed her into three different areas where children had been divided into age groups. In the first, tiny infants were napping in cribs, clad in diapers and light cotton shirts. The occasional woolly head popped up at the sound of our footsteps, but the room was amazingly quiet.

The second ward was for slightly older toddlers. They too were supposed to be napping, but those who hadn't fallen asleep were instantly alert at the sight of us. A few got up and came over, all grins and eyes. My mother, the one who had warned me to keep my distance, was instantly drawn to one little girl who had taken her hand and stood grinning up at her from behind a very runny nose. The third room was for children up to six. After that, there were no more rooms and it was unclear where "old orphans" went. One little boy hung onto the hem of my skirt and tugged anxiously at it for the remainder of the tour. By the time we left, the lady had given me the address and name of someone to speak to in Bridgetown. We continued on our drive excited but "contained." I spent the rest of the day trying not to think too much about what I had just seen.

In the morning, Dad drove us into town. We found the building with no trouble. Since I didn't have an appointment, I was told I would have to wait. Armed with my documents, I settled in while the rest of my family went to shop and look around town. Eventually a dark, trim woman with a pleasant smile came down the hall towards me. "Hello, I'm Vera Small," she said, holding out her hand. "How can I help you?"

I was ushered into her small office and before long had told my story one more time. To my amazement, her response was warm and encouraging. "Well, we do have orphans . . ."

"I know, I saw them."

". . . and our laws are similar to yours, since Barbados and Canada were once part of the British Commonwealth. It shouldn't be too difficult to work out the legal arrangements."

Vera read my home study and spent a long time going through the various letters and endorsements I had gathered along the way. When she was finished she added that if she could find a suitable girl, she would be able to get the paperwork done and have the baby ready to travel in approximately six months. Mentally running down a list of children who were available for placement, she mentioned a three-year-old girl, but thought I would prefer a younger child. There were twins, age two, but they were emotionally disturbed and a huge handful. "I really wouldn't recommend them," she said. "Besides, you really only want one child at present. Later you may decide to have another, but let's just go with one at a time for now."

Vera didn't think there would be much trouble finding an infant in good health. She kept my papers and said she would communicate with Sandra Scarth and me if a suitable child came into care. She promised to review the list of children already in the orphanage and get back to us as soon as possible. Vera took note of where we were staying in Barbados and walked me out of her office in time to meet my parents and Jason, who were back to pick me up. All in all, the visit had gone miraculously well, even though I had expected to meet with a fairly cool reception.

We had been invited to the home of residents of the island that evening. Carol had been an intern at Toronto's Hospital for Sick Children when we got to know her and was now a paediatrician with her own practice. Her husband, Richard, was also a doctor, and they had two young sons. Carol already knew Vera and was very optimistic that she would find me a child. She volunteered to examine the baby herself, and best of all, to keep the child in her own home while the paperwork was being done. We could be sure the baby was healthy and well nurtured until she could travel. I had never felt so comforted; we had tapped the right source at last. Carol promised to get in touch with Vera the next day and I would sign documents saying I agreed to the arrangement before we left for home. We were finally cooking.

Two days later, just as we were getting ready for the beach, a call came for me at the front office. I dropped my towel on the bed and headed to the phone in the reception area. It was Vera Small.

"Miss Cole? I am phoning to let you know we have a ten-day-old infant at the hospital who is available for adoption. Her mother is very young with one child already. She finds it difficult to look after him and planned all along to put this baby up for adoption. Unfortunately, the girl went into early labour while I was on holiday and the nurses didn't understand she wasn't to see the child. When they took the baby in to her mother, the girl didn't know how to tell them of her situation. She left the hospital with her child six days ago, but has had time to rethink her decision. She finds it utterly impossible to handle both children and has returned the infant. I think you will find her a lovely baby and she appears to have been well cared for. I'm sorry this is a little sooner than you expected, but if you like, you could come and see her today and decide if you relate to her."

In a flash I had directions to the hospital and instructions to ask for a Valerie Cranford, who would be there to tell us the baby's history. Vera herself would arrive in forty minutes. I hung up and rushed back to our cottage and my startled family. "Get dressed! Come on! They've got a baby for us to see at the hospital. This is it. This is really it!"

With shaking hands I put a fresh roll of film in the camera. I didn't want to miss recording this first look at my daughter, especially if I wasn't going to be able to see her again for six months. We called Carol to tell her the news, but she was already in the know. In fact, she had been summoned earlier and had already examined the child. "She's quite wonderful," Carol bubbled. "Hurry up, you're going to love her. Remember, I want to look after her until the papers are done."

We piled into the car and found the hospital with no problem. After a short wait, Valerie Cranford appeared. She introduced herself, told us she too was a Canadian, and tried to make small talk while we waited for a nurse to bring the baby to us. I was totally inattentive and wouldn't have cared if she claimed to be from Mars. Vera arrived a few minutes later and finally — finally — a nurse carrying a tiny wrapped bundle came smiling into the room. The baby was handed to me and all at once we were laughing and crying, totally captivated. Dad took pictures while Jason strained to get nearer. All I could see was a tiny heart-shaped face looking up into mine. Infant Ryan had huge eyes, lots of loose, silky, dark brown hair, tight-to-her-head perfect ears, wide nostrils, and a full, sweet mouth that turned up at the corners. Her tiny chin was pointed and deeply dimpled. Her skin was very fair, almost white, and her hands were delicate and long-fingered. I needed to see all of her and unwrapped the tight blanket. I was told she weighed six pounds three ounces, but I did not need to be told she was perfect. The two women beamed for a while and then left us alone. They didn't come back until we had all had a turn holding her and had taken the whole roll of film. When they did return, we sat down to hear details of Infant Ryan's short but eventful life.

Her mother, only sixteen years old, was of average intelligence and had received excellent care and counselling while pregnant. She had been well nourished and seemed concerned that she do all she could to give the baby a good start. The baby's father was white and had been a visitor to the island. Not much more was known. There had never been any intent to keep the baby. The accidental contact between mother and infant after birth had been emotional and confusing for the mother, but now she was again certain she was doing the right thing in giving her child up. I was allowed to hold the baby until we were finished, and when the nurse was finally called back, I held her to my lips and whispered, "I love you and I'm coming back for you, I promise. Don't forget, I'm coming back." I planted one last kiss on her forehead before she was taken away.

Valerie and Vera were smiling. "I take it you feel comfortable with this baby," Valerie said. "Should we go ahead?"

"Please hurry as fast as you can," I urged. I was already wondering how often I could count on Carol to send pictures and how many times I could come for a visit before the courts freed my daughter. I signed release forms for Carol and thanked both women profusely. I wanted to stay, but clearly it was time to leave. We spent the rest of the day celebrating and shopping. We broke the news to Carolyn and Chris back in Toronto as soon as we could get to a telephone.

My sister shrieked into the phone. "What's she like? Tell me everything." And I did, down to the details of her fingernails. We joked about how this little girl would fit right in with our boys.

We even started discussing names and planning how Carolyn would travel to Barbados with me to bring the baby home.

"We took lots of pictures," I told her. "You'll see for yourself in a couple of days." I asked Carolyn to phone Sandra Scarth and tell her what had happened and that she should be expecting a call from Vera shortly. Before I could hang up, the owner of the holiday cottages placed a drink in my hand.

"Congratulations," she said. "I couldn't help overhearing all the calls."

The next two days were heavenly. My mother was worried that I would be sad to leave Barbados and distance myself from the baby. But the relief I was feeling was palpable. Six months wasn't terribly long. She would still be a very young baby when she came to me. Besides, Carol would take good care of her and provide happier surroundings than a hospital or an orphanage could. Just knowing who my daughter was, that she was wonderful and in good hands was enough. I suddenly realized how frightened I had become of all the other unknowns I had been facing. Surely, this was why I had been forced to wait all these months.

─◦─

It was time to go. Fifteen minutes before the taxi was to take us to the airport, the manager summoned me once more to the telephone. It was Valerie Cranford. Her voice was flat. Something was wrong.

"Miss Cole, I'm terribly sorry. I don't know how to begin."

"Just tell me what's happened," I said in a voice empty of expression.

"It's Infant Ryan. She's gone. Her mother just came and took her. She couldn't stand the separation after all. We told her about you and the home you could provide, but she was adamant this time. I'm so sorry. I don't think she will change her mind again."

"Yes she will," I stated flatly. "And when she does, you know how to get in touch with me."

"I know how you must feel. Vera and I are devastated too. We can't help but think everyone involved has lost. We will go on looking for another baby. I'm sure . . ."

But I was beyond hearing. I murmured something by way of goodbye and hung up the phone. It was a minute before I could turn and face going back to my family. When I finally turned from the phone, I met the steady sad gaze of the owner. She understood everything had fallen through and lowered her eyes so as not to watch the first tears fall. I left quickly and got to the bathroom before anyone could see me. I was just washing my face with cold water when Dad knocked on the door.

"Are you all right in there? Who was on the phone?"

I opened the door. "No, I'm not all right. Don't tell Mom and Jason yet. Wait till we get on the plane. Oh, Dad, the baby's gone. Her mother changed her mind and there's nothing I can do."

Dad's long arms were around me in no time. "I'm so sorry," he said. "Don't give up. It is going to happen some day, you'll see."

"I don't think it is, you know? I'm not even sure I want to try anymore. Dad, I really wanted that baby. I promised her . . ."

My big strong father squeezed me even tighter. "I know, I know," he said. When I looked up at him, I saw he was crying too.

Dad and I kept quiet until we were halfway home. My mother was still bubbling about the baby and finally I had to stop her. She and Jason were shocked. We spent the rest of the flight looking like four people who had been to a funeral instead of a holiday.

The worst part was telling Carolyn. She met us at the airport in Dad's car. When we got to the house, pink and white balloons had been tied outside. In the living room stood a crib made up with sheets and blankets, with a white teddy bear tucked under them. Champagne, flowers, and a cake waited on the coffee table.

Carolyn wept when we told her. "Oh, God, why didn't some-one phone me?"

"There wasn't time," I said, untying the first of the balloons. "The crib is beautiful. Thank you. I hope you can take it back."

"No she can't," Dad said. "You're going to need it, if not for this baby, then for another one. Something wasn't right about this time. But it will happen, you mark my words."

7

"I AM THE ONE WHO HAPPEN TO GIVE OUT BABIES"

In the weeks that followed the Infant Ryan fiasco there was a flurry of letter writing. Sandra Scarth was contacted by the powers that be in Barbados. Carol wrote to apologize for the inept handling of the whole affair. She had complained bitterly to Vera and Valerie for offering a child whose mother had not yet lived through the ten-day grace period after signing her child away. The two women were chagrined and sorry. Both sent notes expressing regrets and promising to keep me in mind for another child — one who was well and truly available for placement. I answered everyone, always expressing the hope that somehow Infant Ryan's mother would have another change of heart, but as days turned into weeks, I knew this would never happen.

Sometimes I would imagine a young girl sitting on a stool in the sun, dandling a tiny baby, clean and sweet-smelling and dressed in pink. The girl would return her baby's smile and plant a tender kiss on her forehead, right where mine had been. Remembering how she had almost missed this and every other moment, the young woman would hold the child close and cherish her all the more. Then the image would fade. Maybe this was right. Maybe this time things had worked out the way they were supposed to. Still, something akin to bitterness rested beneath that hope.

It was a while before I could take the holiday film in to be developed. Ironically, the pictures we took of Infant Ryan that afternoon turned out poorly. The images were fuzzy and grainy — a memory already dissolving — as if they knew they should hurry away and not be part of my story. It didn't matter. I would never need photographs to remember that face.

Far from making me see how close I had come and how possible things might be, this last miss had changed me. Now I was still going through the motions, but I no longer believed in an outcome. I felt like I had been caught up in an eternal game that would always have beginnings but no completion. Every time I entered into another attempt or followed another lead, I could almost imagine some gleeful, malevolent force twisting the path, throwing up roadblocks, warping the outcome. In order to keep on playing I kept my distance, always trying to remind myself not to count on anything. Fill in the papers, get the signatures, send the details. I did it all, time and time again. I was becoming practised with beginnings; it was the endings I couldn't master. Months sped by and suddenly it was the end of another year.

It was little wonder, then, that when Carolyn came home from work one evening, I barely took her seriously as she began to tell me about an interesting contact she'd made.

"I have this friend at work. Her name is Malaya Mendoza and she's really nice. She's from the Philippines and she's going home for Christmas. Apparently her father didn't understand why she wanted to come here instead of staying at home. She wants to go back and make things up if she can."

Carolyn couldn't possibly have missed the dubious expression on my face, but she ignored it and continued quickly. "Anyway, she says her mother knows someone who has placed children with families abroad from time to time, some rich socialite or something. Malaya has volunteered to take your home study with her and promises to look this woman up for you. It might be worth a try."

I was almost annoyed with Carolyn. This was the kind of thing we had done at the outset. There was no structure to it, no safety net — in my mind there was no chance it could work. It was so nebulous and casual, all I could see was danger.

"Who is this woman?" I asked. "Does Malaya know her well or is this friend of her mother's really a friend of a friend? And where does a rich socialite come up with orphans? Is there an agency involved or a lawyer or anything legal? I don't know, Carolyn, it sounds a little crazy to me."

"Well it might be, but why not find out? I really don't think Malaya would suggest anything illegal. She said this woman works through a lawyer and the courts. It couldn't hurt to send your papers with a letter and see what Malaya comes back with."

I didn't want to hurt Carolyn's feelings and in a way I guessed she was right, but visions of my lunch in Burlington began to flit through my head. I didn't put much time into the covering letter I wrote that night. Carolyn took it and the rest of my papers to work the next day, and I didn't give the matter another thought.

Christmas came and went, and early in January Malaya returned to work. Her visit home had been very successful. Her parents had a better understanding of why she wanted to be independent and there had been a reconciliation. The holidays had been a whirlwind of social activity, though, and unfortunately there hadn't been time to do anything with my papers.

I wasn't surprised. I wasn't even disappointed. But there was more. Malaya told Carolyn that she had left the package with her mother who had promised to pass it along to her friend early in the New Year.

Carolyn decided it was time I met Malaya, and invited her to dinner at her place. I liked Malaya right from the start. She was interesting, vivacious, and had a good sense of humour. She also seemed very responsible. When I asked her about the mystery woman, she spoke quite openly.

"Actually, I don't know her all that well, but my parents have known her for quite a while. She has a lot of money and I think she supports hospitals and orphanages quite a bit. Every now and then, she gets involved in placing a baby for adoption." Malaya settled on the couch. "I know a couple of times she has sent children to homes outside of the Philippines, to England I think. She works through a lawyer and the courts and, according to my mother, goes to quite a bit of trouble to complete everything properly."

"What does she charge for doing all this?" I asked.

"I think she asks for enough money to cover her own and the legal expenses, but nothing more. She's not in it for cash; she has lots."

I was becoming more interested, and we spent the rest of the evening talking and getting to know each other better. Before Malaya left that night she told me that her parents had taken an interest in my story. Rather embarrassed, she added that her father was "a pretty well-known lawyer in the Philippines" and that if anything came of this, he would take an active role in helping to expedite the process. "I've never said much about it, but really, my father is not without influence. I truly think if my mother's friend has a baby, you would be in good hands."

"Good," I said with some relief. "The last thing I want to do is get involved in anything underhanded." I thanked Malaya sincerely before she left, feeling a glimmer of interest growing into a bothersome ray of hope.

Carolyn had a very pleased look on her face as she closed the door behind Malaya. "Well, what do you think?" she asked.

"Sounds good. We'll see."

—◦—

We didn't hear another word until March 20. I was keenly aware that it was Infant Ryan's first birthday. She would be learning to walk by now. Somehow, I missed seeing the significance in the timing of the letter Carolyn brought home from work with her that evening. Malaya had received it the day before and passed it on. It was the first link in a long chain of letters that followed. With each correspondence, I lost my reserve by degrees until once again, I was vulnerable to optimism. It all began with this one letter to Malaya that Carolyn now held out to me. Many more would follow.

March 10, 1980

Dear Malaya,

I'm sure you will be surprise why a letter in my name. I am the daughter of Rose D. Rodrigez and she gave me your letter about your friend who is interested in adopting a baby. You see I am the one who happen to give out babies almost eleven years ago. I started with the child of my sister and since then I would be getting from a poor mother who cannot afford to support her baby and I would give them to a couple who can very well afford them. So if your friend is really interested in having a baby I have one who is still on the family way and she promised to give me her baby be it a boy or a girl. You can give this letter to your friend. To give you an idea of the amount I have spend to the baby boy that I gave to a

British family cost us around P 19,000.00 that include the amount I gave the mother, the Attorney's fees who worked on the adoption papers, and the passport and ticket of the baby. So if your friend is really interested she has to send me her passport picture and passport documents, her income tax return, and her properties there to show the judge here that she can afford to adopt a baby. The lawyer will go to the judge and have the hearing set. Your mama can always be the one to testify or tell the judge your friend is of good moral character. Well, that is all and when the baby is ready to send to Canada, your friend will just come here and bring the baby there.

Well, I hope to hear from you soon. Ma is too old to thinks of these matters and so when she got your letter she gave it to me.

Sorry for the delay in answering but I've been busy with the children and their activities plus the work at the office.

Regards to you and your friend.

Always,
Emilia Sanches

P.S. The baby can also stay in our house while awaiting for the papers. The last baby that we sent to Singapore stayed with our family for six months.

March 20, 1980
Mrs. Emilia Sanches
Metro Manila, Philippines

Dear Mrs. Sanches,

I have in hand your letter of March 10 to Malaya, our mutual friend. I am very encouraged by it and delighted to think I may be able to receive a child from you. I am trying to stay calm and not get too excited just yet. I have had other good possibilities before that didn't work out because of adoption regulations against single parents in some countries. If you are certain, or can find out, that this is no problem in your country I would be most relieved and grateful.

You mentioned in your letter that you know a woman who intends to offer her baby up for adoption. If you could supply me with more information as to when the baby is due to be born, some background on the parents, the age of the mother, and her general state of health, etc., again I would be grateful.

I believe my home study done by the government's official adoption agency here in Ontario is a very complete and positive one. My preference for a girl child is stated quite clearly in the study, but I would like to state that should this woman have a baby boy, I would be just as interested in adopting him. At the outset I was asked my preference as to the child's sex as we thought we would be dealing with children who were already born, where a definite choice would have to be made. I do understand that in an arrangement of this sort, one takes what comes along just as any natural parent does. My only concern is that the baby is normal and healthy. This has been a very strong stipulation all along and one that I still feel is important. I assume the baby would be thoroughly examined by medical doctors and that I would have some assurances that all was well before coming to the Philippines.

I hope you believe that I am most anxious to pursue this actively but I have had enough experience with this to want to avoid problems if at all possible. I draw to your attention, though I know it is in my study, that I am not a Roman Catholic. If this is going to be a stumbling block now or later, please do not let me hope otherwise. If you feel that we are still in a position to proceed, I promise to do all I can to supply you with any necessary documents to expedite a legal adoption.

On a more personal note, I want you to know that this has been my heart's greatest desire for many years now and I am deeply committed to bringing it about. The child who is eventually placed in my care will have the very best I can offer and it will be given with great happiness.

I am most eager to hear from you again and thank you in advance for any information you can supply. Even if you find that this adoption is not possible after all, I am very grateful for your interest.

Sincerely,
Kathryn Cole

April 11, 1980
Ms. Sandra Scarth
The Children's Aid Society
15 Huntley Street, Toronto

Hi Sandra,

Thanks for your call this morning. Enclosed are the letters we discussed for your files. After speaking with you I think it would be best if you would send Mrs. Sanches an updated copy of my home study on Children's Aid letterhead and perhaps a covering letter if you think it would help. I am really most anxious for this to work if at all possible and would appreciate it going as soon as you can manage.

Thanks for your help,
Kathryn

April 16, 1980
Mrs. Emilia Sanches
Metro Manila, The Philippines

Dear Mrs. Sanches,

Enclosed is our updated adoption study as requested by Miss Kathryn Cole. We have great confidence in her ability to care for a child both financially and emotionally. She also has the support of her family and friends.

Although the study states a preference for a girl, she is equally interested in a boy at this time. Thank you for your kind consideration of Miss Cole's application.

Yours sincerely,
Sandra Scarth (Mrs.)
Social Worker, Adoption Service
Toronto East Branch
c.c. Miss Cole

May 7, 1980

Dear Kathie,

My esposo and myself have been giving much thoughts to your request. It is my esposo's opinion that we should proceed with as much haste as possible as he says you are in very desperate condition from the sound of your letters. I have a change of plan in mind as the baby of the girl I know is not due yet for another months and may even be a boy. There is another baby girl who I am sending her photo now. She is one years old already and this is her birthday picture taken in the house of my brother. If you like this baby girl you can just tell me and we will go ahead and get the papers ready for you. So don't forget to

*just let me know and I will start the Attorney to get going.
All together we might have the hearing in four months if
we hurry. This baby is staying in the home of my brother
since her mother was very poor and just cannot keep her.
So Kathie, I will wait to hear from you as to this little girl
whose name is Mari. My phone number is here if you
want to hurry faster than the mails.*

Always,
Emilia

May 14, 1980

Dear Emilia,

*I was delighted to speak to you last night and to hear
that everything appears to be going well with the adoption
plans. I don't think you can imagine the excitement those
two photos have caused in my family. The baby is absolutely beautiful. Everyone is afraid to hope she will be ours in
a few months. The wait will be very difficult, I can assure
you. I have already phoned Malaya and she is very happy
to think she was able to help by giving me your name. By
now I know you have the copies of my passport and income
tax return. I will, as you requested, send a letter giving you
power of attorney for the purpose of the adoption as soon
as my lawyer writes it up. At that time I will also enclose a
letter from my bank manager listing my holdings. Despite
your assurances that religion is not an issue, it continues
to nag at me in case the judge sees it as a problem. I have
asked a friend to send a personal recommendation that
may help only if the question arises. If you need anything
else, please let me know and I will send it.*

KATHRYN COLE

I will not start the immigration papers yet as you no doubt know when it is best to do that. I will await your instructions on that matter.

I want to repeat what I said on the phone. I will definitely come in four months or so for the court date if you think there is an advantage or that it would speed things along. Anything we can do to take short cuts would be wonderful as I am very eager to bring Mari to her new home as soon as possible. In the meantime I will try to be patient!

I do not know yet what I will name her as it will have to be something very pretty and special. If it is possible to send more pictures soon I would appreciate it very much.

For now I will close with warmest regards and deepest gratitude for the help you are giving the baby and me. Please ask your brother to give Mari an extra hug from me. I am eager to meet you all and hope it won't be long before I do.

Sincerely,
Kathie

May 20, 1980
Mrs. Emilia Sanches,
Metro Manila, The Philippines

Re: Kathryn D. Cole

Dear Mrs. Sanches:
First of all, allow me to introduce myself as the Chancellor of the Archdiocese of Toronto and Auxiliary Bishop to His Eminence, Gerald Cardinal Carter, Archbishop of Toronto.

I am happy to address a word to you because Miss Cole has spoken to me of the conversations she has had with you quite recently with reference to the adoption of an infant girl.

The Coles are long-standing and appreciated friends of mine, and I have no hesitation in recommending Kathryn, of whose high reputation in the community I am well aware. I am happy to add this word of commendation because I believe that the infant you may be able to propose for adoption would receive a very warm and wonderful welcome in Kathryn's home and care.

I can also put your mind at ease as to any question you might have relative to the religious upbringing of this infant, should the infant be already a baptized Roman Catholic. I know that Kathryn would honour this commitment and that her wide circle of friends, so many of whom are Catholics, would be of assistance to her.

I wish to assure you that the cooperation you have already shown is most appreciated, and that any consideration you may be able to show in facilitating and expediting this adoption procedure would be likewise appreciated.

With every best wish,
(Most Rev.) Leonard J. Wall, D.D.,
Auxiliary Bishop of Toronto,
Chancellor.

June 19, 1980

Dear Kathie,

Here are more pictures of Mari taken by my brother. As of now she is still staying with my brother as I have the

*new baby which was born a boy, so it is good fate has save
the girl for you. The only information I know is that her
mother was a friend of my auntie. My auntie was the one
who gave her to me after she promise the mother that the
baby will be taken care of by her friends, as the mother is
too poor to bring her up. Now my auntie is very ill with a
stroke she suffer last January. So as for the family background that you were asking me I really can't give much.
I just hope and pray that all these children I give out for
adoption will turn out to be good children of God and
that the foster parents will not be disappointed in them
when they grow up.*

*Now I have your power of attorney giving me the
authority to represent you in court so that you don't have
to come here all the way during the hearing. You can just
come here when all the papers are ready and Mari has her
passport already. I just hope that we will not have a hard
time as just last month the racket of selling babies has
been exposed in our local newspapers so all the judge having the hearings on adoption are really very careful. I just
hope that everything will come out all right with our Mari.*

*When I visited her three weeks ago Mari did not like to
go with me anymore as she has been used to the helpers of
my brother. So I prefer that the sooner you get her the better so that her personality will get adjusted to your personality and you will not have a hard time. Maybe I will
be able to bring her here soon so she will get used to more
people. My brother has two daughters only while we have
five and we stay in a compound.*

*I am really happy that the babies I have given out are
all happy in their respective homes. Before I could give
them as gifts but now with the high costs of hospital bills
and preparation of the papers I really cannot afford not*

to charge my expenses. So my only contribution will be preparing their papers, going to the court to be witness, and talking to the lawyers. I hope you will understand. And taking care of them while the babies are in our house are the things we can do for these innocent children. As of now Mari will be the 15th baby I'm helping and I hope and pray they will have a happy future with you.

Well, let's hope that everything will turn out well and for the best for everyone. Thanks and hope to meet you in person some day.

Regards to your parents,
Emilia

June 21, 1980

Dear Kathie,

Well what a nice surprise to get your cheery letter with the good news of little Mari and the pictures of her. I will be glad to welcome her and have her name on the family tree. She really looks a cute little doll and we do hope all comes through for you and we hope if she comes you will both find much happiness together. But Kathie, you will have to have patience as it will be a big change for her and she will be a little stranger in a big strange land. However, I know this will all be worked out in time. So my dear, I have my knees crossed as I sit here, wishing you good luck. You sure have waited a long time. As my mother always said, everything comes to those who wait, so maybe this time the waiting will come to something.

Well my dear there is not much news from here. I got your mom's letter and I will answer it next. Really dear, I should have written you sooner but I have not been up to it, or anything else, this past couple of weeks. The doctor was in to see me and says everything is steady, so I guess I have much to be thankful for, but some days I really feel low. Just let me sleep says I. Your Aunt Phyllis tries so hard to fix me something I like, but nothing tastes as it should. I know I am getting skinny but that's good for the old knees. I do look awful though. Ha.

I must be closing now. Just wanted to let you know I got the pictures. The time will pass quickly so you can be off to get her for your very own. Keep smiling and maybe, just maybe, this time all your dreams will come true. I'll be sure to stick around long enough to see that. Ha, ha.

Love as always,
Gram

By now I was so involved in keeping the momentum going that I had lost interest in all else. I went to work every day and spent the rest of my time writing letters and getting the required papers. Many nights were spent waiting until it was late enough to place a call to the other side of the world and chat with the woman who was so confident she could handle everything. The arrival of Mari's first snapshots had revealed a tiny girl, delicate and winsome. There was a quality to the expression on the baby's face. She stood in one picture, leaning on the back cushions of a sofa. Her big round eyes were solemn and wary. Despite her pleasant surroundings and the assortment of toys strewn about, there was never a trace of a smile in any of the pictures I received through all the months of letter writing.

This little girl whose photo I held in my hands was in need of someone and I was certain that someone was meant to be me.

8

"WHAT DO YOU MEAN,
TWO CHILDREN?"

Emilia's thirst for legal paperwork was insatiable. I spent a very long lunch hour running from bank to lawyer and post office on July 25 obtaining further bank statements and notarizations in order to fill the demands of her latest cable. These were needed, she said, so that a hearing date could be set. There was no time to waste and I managed to pop everything in the mail and be back behind my desk by 1:45. Just as I was beginning to concentrate, the phone rang. The second I recognized Sandra Scarth's voice I launched into my newest update. Sandra waited till I was finished, but just.

"That's nice," she commented hastily, "but listen to me. Something amazing has come up. I was sitting in a meeting at Charles Street with Helen Allen and Victoria Leach — Victoria's the adoption coordinator for Ontario. Anyway, a call came for Victoria from Ottawa. They wanted to know if Ontario could place four refugee children from Cambodia. Right now the children are in a border camp in Thailand, but things are deteriorating and the authorities are trying to move these four unaccompanied minors out of danger. If we can find homes for them, they'll come within the next month. Kathryn, you should have been here. The second Victoria told us, all three of us just looked at each other and said your name in unison. Because these babies aren't coming through regular channels, the Children's Aid Society will not be appointed their legal guardian. Therefore we're freer to place the children in homes of our choosing. This is the break we've been waiting for."

Sandra was right. But now I was committed to another situation. I sat thunderstruck while Sandra waited for the news to sink in. She must have been terribly disappointed when no cheers went up.

"But Sandra, I hardly know what to say. You know what I've been working on in the Philippines. Things are looking better all the time. What am I supposed to do about Mari, just bail out?"

Sandra was firm when she finally found her voice. "Now you listen to me, Kathryn Cole. We've been working on this forever, and we've both gone through hell. I'm telling you, this is real and definite. Unless these babies die first, they are coming to homes in Ontario. We have hundreds of people who would take them, but we're offering you one first. You don't have any idea of what will happen in a court in Manila; surely you've been through enough to realize that. My strong advice is to take your bird in the hand. You can always decide what to do about the other baby later."

Sandra's logic hit home. She was right. "What do you know about the four babies?" I asked, beginning to catch the excitement.

Sandra, with a huge sigh of relief, jumped right in.

"Well, one is a boy, so that one's out. The oldest of the three girls is somewhere around eighteen months. Her name is Bunh

Sun. She came into the camp in mid-March and has had ear infections, but that's pretty common to children in poor conditions. I
suggest you take her because she is a toddler. With your being
single and having to work, it might be best if you didn't have
diapers and infancy to deal with. What do you think?"

"I don't know. What about the others?"

"The next baby down is somewhere around a year old and the
youngest is about seven months."

"What's her name?" I asked, getting more excited by the
second.

"Let's see, I have Victoria's notes here," Sandra said, ruffling
through some papers. "Yes, here she is, Sla Line. No one knows
what she was called by her parents. This child was found on a
road near the border. There were bodies, perhaps of her family,
nearby. She was picked up by a nun who came upon her and
carried her into the camp. She has been in the children's
hospital there ever since. That was in February and they guessed
then that the baby was about six weeks old. That would give her
a December birthdate. Oh, it says she has been cared for by three
house mothers, but now the latest one is unable to continue. Her
photo has been circulated in villages nearby and in the camp,
but no one can identify her. There's nothing more — just that
all four of the babies have dysentery, ear infections and are
malnourished. Other than that, they have been deemed well
enough to travel."

There was no need to go any further. Bunh Sun might be the
one Sandra recommended, but I had settled on Sla Line, the
youngest of the three girls.

"Are you certain?"

"Yes, Sandra, I'm certain. Sla Line. The younger the better,
remember?"

Relieved that I had at least come to my senses enough to
understand the importance of what was happening, Sandra

agreed. "OK, done! I'm putting you down for Sla Line. The babies will be arriving in August on either the 15th, 27th, or 29th. I'll phone you later when I get a confirmed date and flight number. There will likely be paperwork to do."

"Naturally," I laughed, remembering, with slight discomfort, the papers I had just so hastily dropped in the mailbox, destination the Philippines.

I could almost see the happiness spread across Sandra's face. "Congratulations, Mom," she said before the line went dead in my hands.

I was still looking into the receiver when my assistant, Lesley, walked past my open door. "What's wrong?" she asked with concern.

"Nothing. Nothing's wrong. It's just that I'm going to end up with two children here, that's all."

"What do you mean, two children?"

"I just got a call about a baby. She's coming within the month. It's not Mari, it's another one. I said yes. I'm telling you, Lesley, I'm going to have two babies, not one."

Her face turned smoky and her voice was full of disdain. "Don't be ridiculous. You can't have two children! Do you want to be wiped right off the map?"

The comment may have been meant in my own best interest, but, effectively, the gauntlet had just been thrown down. Nobody ever tells me I can't do something without a fight. There would be much soul searching to come with regard to Mari. But Lesley had just pushed me one very large step closer to believing I not only could, but also wanted, to have these two children. Rather like someone who has received the news that she is about to have twins, I had simply been momentarily taken aback. These babies were both mine and I was beginning to adjust to the number two already. Other people had two children — it wasn't that much of a stretch.

"No," I told her, an incredulous grin spreading from ear to ear, "I don't want to be wiped off the map, and don't worry, I won't be."

Lesley sniffed as if it wasn't worth talking to one as mad as I. She would never say another word on the topic and very soon she would become enthusiastic about Sla Line's arrival, but for now there wasn't a hint of understanding for the situation. I guess that was to be expected. After all, it wasn't Lesley's purse that Mari's pictures had been nestled in for the past few months.

The department quickly became aware of the news and there was genuine elation from the rest of the staff that afternoon. They too had suffered the ups and downs of the past years and they all, except Lesley, felt a sensation of reprieve.

Uncharacteristically, I didn't pick up the phone and call my sister or parents. I hugged the secret to myself for the remainder of the afternoon, delirious with anticipation of this "definite" event. No one had ever used that word yet, least of all Sandra. Shadows of self-doubt flickered ever so briefly during the remainder of that workday, but I bravely pushed them back. There was too much light in my being to allow the darkness of reality to gain a foothold. Sandra was right. There would be time to decide about everything later. Mari's image stayed sharp and clear as I set to wondering how this new person in my life would look. I could picture her body; it would be smaller than Mari's. It was her face that eluded me. Only one more month and I would know.

On the way home, I stopped and bought champagne and flowers. Once in the car, I realized with a thump I had chosen pink carnations and white baby's breath — the same bouquet Carolyn had waiting for us on our homecoming from Barbados. But I drove on, even managing to dismiss the fact that this might be one more false start. By the time I reached home I was bursting with news.

"Dust off the crib," I shouted as I entered the house. "We're going to need it after all."

My mother turned from her work at the kitchen counter, with a look I'll never forget. She dropped the knife when she saw me and came hurrying down the hall. Dad threw down the newspapers and Chris and Jason came running. Carolyn was coming up the street from the bus stop and arrived just in time for the first glass of champagne to be slipped into her hand.

The celebration that night was without reserve. From experience we should have known better, but we no longer had the energy to hold back. Somehow each of us sensed we had suffered all the setbacks that had been stacked and waiting for us. They had been depleted at last and now we could finally savour the bubbles and roll that delicious word "definite" over our tongues. We sat, all six of us, happy to be together and aware that we were not all together — yet. Mari was mentioned, but Carolyn quickly agreed with Sandra. There would be time to decide later. First, we would see who this new baby was and how she was. After that I would know what to do. We did that night what many people do when there really is no choice to make. We resigned ourselves to believing that everything past and present was providential. There had been a reason for everything, after all.

With each day that passed we were one day closer to completion. The time wasn't empty. I had some running to do, back and forth to Immigration Canada, so that the baby's papers would be ready on time. And there was a bedroom to prepare. I painted and papered and picked up a second used crib from Cathy and Shaun, who had recommended me. The crib was old and the paint had turned chalky, but with a weekend's work, it stood gleaming and fresh, with a new mattress and stencilling on both the head and footboards. Carolyn's smaller crib would go up in Mom's room. We would need one in both places. I bought a small chest of drawers at a garage sale and refinished it to match the crib. In the days that followed, when I wasn't painting or working frantically in the office, I was busy reading or writing letters, shopping for supplies, and generally giving in to the expectation that had long ago abandoned me. One of the first things I had to do was extricate myself from the efforts being made on my behalf by Sandra Simpson. The possibility of facing two children was daunting enough. Three would be out of the question and I didn't want to run the risk of hearing about, or deciding on, any more sad stories.

Ms. Sandra Simpson
Families For Children
July 29/80

Dear Sandra,

It is with great happiness that I am finally able to write this note to you. Last Friday Sandra Scarth phoned to tell me that four very young Cambodian babies will be arriving in Canada near the end of August and that I will be given a seven-month-old girl. My feet are only now beginning to touch the ground.

I wanted to send this right away so that you will remove my name from your list. I sincerely appreciate your efforts to help so many needy children find families in need of them. I hope the enclosed cheque will express that gratitude in a slightly more useful way. I only regret that I turned out to be one of your more difficult cases. Regardless, I hope you can share my joy and accept my wishes for good health, happiness, and continued success in the future.

Sincerely,
Kathryn Cole

July 31, 1980

Dear Miss Cole,

Re: Proposed Immigration and Adoption of Sla Line (F), born December, 1979, in Cambodia

We have today informed the Immigration Division in Metropolitan Toronto that we have no objection to the transfer of the above named child into your home in Ontario.

The final decision concerning the granting of an immigrant visa to the child will be made by Employment and Immigration Canada.

A copy of our letter of approval is enclosed for your information.

Yours very truly,
Alan Leslie,
A Director of Child Welfare

August 2, 1980

Dear Kathie,

Well, we got the good news from your mom when she arrived last night. We sure hope this is the one and we are so happy for you. So now you may have two little girls. Well, like the saying goes, on a streetcar there's always room for one more. Anyway, if such is the case we know you'll be able to handle the job.

Your mom and Jason have just gone down to the lake for a swim. I have not been down to the waterfront yet but look at the lake from the cottage and it looks lovely. Your mom says if all goes well with the baby you may try to bring her down before we have to close up here. It will be great to see her, I do hope all is well and she will soon adjust. With all the love she is bound to get she should thrive.

Well, I must go. Your mother has promised something good to tempt me with for dinner. I hope the weather will stay good so we can be here when you come. I have my knees crossed for number 4 great grandchild coming up.

From your Ever-loving Gram XXX

On Friday, August 15, I received another call from Sandra Scarth. She had great and not-so-great news. Fortunately she started with the great part. "I have a date and flight time. Have you got a pen?"

I did, and wrote, "August 27, CP flight 80, Terminal 1, 20:40." Even as I wrote the words, I couldn't believe this small slip of white scrap paper was marked with the information I had been waiting for all my life. It was as if someone had finally unwrapped the surprise package that had been given to me at birth but had been left to sit unopened until this moment.

"The provincial authorities are sending a representative, Mary Jane Turner, this Tuesday morning. She will meet with a nurse in Thailand and together they will bring the four babies back with them on the 27th. You should call your doctor and make an appointment to have the child examined as soon after her arrival as possible. She needs a certificate for the Medical Officer of Health. Bring a cheque to cover the baby's and a portion of the escorts' expenses. Be sure you have some identification, too, because Mary Jane doesn't know you."

"Won't you be there?" I asked.

"I'll try, but right now it doesn't look good. I may have to be out of town that week." Then Sandra dropped a tiny bombshell. It would have unsettled me much more than it did, except that she seemed so calm and certain that this was just a formality and not a snag.

"Now, there's something else," she said. "It makes no difference, really, but the United Nations is concerned about their role in all of this. Because their mandate is to reunify families, they are very nervous about letting the four babies go for adoption. They have already exhausted all hope of finding the families of these children and they know there is no hope. Still, they are not in the business of adoption. The way around this is to allow the children out of the camp and into Ontario on a refugee guardianship. That means the baby can stay with you, but you cannot apply to adopt her immediately. In a year or so, you will be able to, but not yet. Mary Jane has been designated as the supervisor for a year. After that you will have full control of the baby's future."

"Sandra, I couldn't stand it if I had this baby for even a day and had to send her back. How certain are they about her family?"

"They wouldn't let her go at all if there was any chance that there was a living relative, even a distant one. The situation in Cambodia is chaotic and this camp alone holds 160,000 people. This baby is unidentifiable now. She was lost at six weeks of age and is now around about eight months old. And possession is nine-tenths of the law. Once the child is here and being well taken care of by you, no one would be very eager to send her back to such dangerous conditions. This is simply the way to get her to safety and shouldn't worry you for a minute. I've just spoken to Immigration Canada and they will accept the baby on an unaccompanied minor program. You can apply for guardianship and the baby can be covered under your health insurance and will qualify as your dependent. It's going to be fine."

I had already taken so many chances and leaps into the unknown. This last one didn't make me happy but if I had to agree, I had to. I looked down at the paper on my desk. My pen was still poised above the words "August 27, CP flight 80, Terminal 1, 20:40." "All right," I said, as I added three exclamation marks. "Done!"

"Good. That's a week Wednesday at 8:40 p.m. Don't be late. And Kathryn, I know how you must be feeling. I'm dying to see this little girl myself."

Two days later, as if to lay claim to Mari's position of first child, the following message arrived.

CNCP Telepost AUG 17 0931 EST

Dear Kathie,

Received all your papers. Everything needed now in hand. Our lawyer on vacation. Will keep you posted on Mari's papers.

Regards, Emilia

9

"THIS IS SLA LINE. GOOD LUCK. SHE'S A LIVE ONE."

I knew the moment I woke up on August 27 that it was going to be a scorcher of a day. I had spent the night tossing and sweating — mine was a mind on the loose, out of control, and no amount of reason or happiness was going to contain it through the dark hours of the night. Half-dreams came and went, interrupted by the brief spells of wakefulness. But with the morning light, my senses gained control again and dismissed the anxiety of not being able to measure up to my new role. Far from feeling tired, I arrived at work full of energy and spent most of the day writing lists and getting things in order for my assistant so that she could take over with little difficulty. Lesley looked like a lamb being led to slaughter but even that didn't bother me much. She had already had her vacation and I had done double duty then. I was only planning two weeks off now, in case I needed the remaining two weeks of my personal holidays for Mari. There was still no adoption leave.

By the afternoon I detected more than one furtive glance from colleagues and noticed how conversations stopped abruptly every time I turned a corner or entered a room. That was when the first of the cramps started, signalling a build-up of nerves that even I could no longer ignore. Well aware of the company's tradition of gift giving at weddings and baby arrivals, I called Lesley into my office.

"Lesley," I said, "I don't want to be a wet blanket, but if anyone is planning a presentation in the lobby, please stop it right now. I would far rather wait until I know the baby is here than have to make explanations to the whole company if something goes wrong."

By the look on Lesley's face, I knew I had guessed correctly. "Please," I begged.

Not another word was spoken, and I continued to work, only stopping whenever the phone rang. Miraculously, the call that would have dashed all hope never came. I had numerous visits from friends wishing me well and making me promise to bring the baby in to show them as soon as I could. Someone brought flowers, and by the time I left that day, I was in a high state of excitement. Once out of the office air conditioning, I couldn't believe how hot it was.

At the airport, we had all stood perspiring, waiting. Until the shout, "There's Mary Jane. She's got four!" went up, I had not allowed myself to really believe that we had made it. And now as the little girl with wet panties continued to cry, the door swung open one last time.

The instant I saw them, my feet began to work. Wobbly knees, sick stomach, and any awareness of the heat vanished. Walking towards us were three women carrying four babies. One was a flight attendant with two small infants, another was a Thai nurse, the third had to be Mary Jane.

That's all that registered before my gaze connected and

locked on the most alert pair of eyes I had ever seen. They were wide set and dominated a porcelain-perfect face. The features were framed by a mop of dark hair, enough to have been cut and shaped with a fringe of thick bangs across the forehead. The baby was being carried by Mary Jane, face out, legs dangling. She was wearing a light, pale blue cotton dress and she was, bar none, the most beautiful sight I had ever seen. Tiny and doll-like, her expression contradicted her delicacy. The wisdom of ages was written on her face and she had honed in on me like a heat-seeking missile. Despite the confusion of everything going on around her, she studied my face. "So that's who you are," she seemed to communicate. "I've been waiting so long. What kept you?"

"Oh, God," I prayed. "Help me look at the others. She can't be the one. How could they give me anything so exquisite?" I tried to tear my eyes away. I tried to look at the other three babies, but the best I could do was manage to see peripherally. The larger toddler was being handed to the family with the little girl and the wet daddy. She was crying along with her new big sister, while the rest of the group was laughing, rejoicing, comforting both children. *Bunh Sun*, I thought, happy that I liked the family she would go to. To the left I managed to catch a glimpse of a still, sleeping bundle wrapped in blue, being handed to a young couple. The boy had been accounted for. There were only two left. Somewhere a little farther away, I heard a woman sob, "Oh, how beautiful," and all the time the child I was watching was being carried closer to me.

"Are you Kathryn Cole?" the weary voice behind her asked.

"Yes," I replied.

"Well, this is Sla Line. Good luck. She's a live one."

I barely had time to raise my arms and suddenly I was holding my little girl. Even as I squeezed her tight, she pulled her head back so she could keep looking into my eyes. For a moment, the tiny mouth puckered at the corners and I was sure she was going to cry. Then, with remarkable resolve, she decided crying was not the thing to do on such an occasion. Instead she nodded her head once, very definitely, in a wordless greeting. This little soul was far braver than I. Tears streamed down my face as my family closed in around us in a huge embrace.

I had already memorized the size and weight and feel of her by the time my mother held out her arms to take her. I gave her up reluctantly. The baby stared at me the whole time. Only when Dad approached did she turn to him and nod her head in an abrupt hello. We all laughed. One of the airport passersby exclaimed, "Oh, look! They're giving away babies!"

"Like hell they are," I thought as I took mine back. She was surprisingly light despite the apparent chubbiness of her torso. Later I would learn that the roundness was caused from malnutrition. But hungry or not, this baby held herself very straight and I could sense a comforting strength in her even if she was small. Once back in my arms, Sla Line settled in comfortably. I rubbed and patted her back, kissed her, bounced her, and was remarkably pleased to feel her warm hand on my neck, patting me back in time to the beat. Finally, after leaving us alone for a few minutes, Mary Jane was back. Grinning, she handed me a small bag. At home I would find a soiled diaper and dress and an empty bottle: the sum total of Sla Line's earthly possessions. Carolyn held the baby while I produced identification and signed the documents with a shaky hand. A Red Cross Visa was given to me and I handed over the certified cheque for the airfare. Then Mary Jane gave me a half-filled bottle of milky substance. Anxious to keep feeding the baby what she was used to, I asked what it contained.

"I haven't the slightest idea," Mary Jane said, "But that's the last of it, anyway. Just feed her whatever she'll take for now. She's hungry. Did you make a doctor's appointment?"

"Yes."

"Good. I'll be in touch in a few days to see how you're doing. Oh, I almost forgot. I took pictures of the refugee camp so you could see where she was and I will make you a set if you like. And here; I bought one of these for each of the children. It's for good luck. She should have something from her homeland."

Mary Jane handed me a carved wooden elephant with white tusks and she wished us luck one more time. She disappeared into the arms of her own family who had come to welcome her home.

And that was it. Just like that we were on our own, still celebrating at the top of the escalator. Chris ran to a pay phone and called Jean, Vern, and their daughter Betty. Our neighbours were on standby and waiting to hear from the airport that all was well. I heard Chris chirp into the receiver, "She's here all right, and the cutest thing you ever saw. She's got lots of hair and, Aunt Jean, tall people and big noses don't run in the family anymore. Get ready, we're on our way home."

My father hated to pull himself away, but someone had to go and get the car. "Wait inside," he ordered, as he started off. "Don't let the baby catch a draft."

I had to laugh. The poor little girl was soaked with perspiration. Her dress was limp and clinging to her, but she seemed to be enjoying all the attention anyway. We dutifully waited inside as we were told, but after twenty minutes, Dad still hadn't come. Finally, sporting an embarrassed smile, he pulled up outside. "I was so nervous, I forgot to pay attention to where I parked the car," he confessed.

All the way home, the baby was passed from one to the other. She was calm, but obviously amazed by the car and the movements of the lights and passing scenery. This child had never had a car ride and she was determined to learn all about it during this first occasion. Sitting on Carolyn's lap she nodded again, which brought peals of laughter from the boys. That was when we witnessed the first smile. Two pearls of bottom teeth were barely visible above the gum line as the tiny cheerio-sized mouth spread and lit the whole car with a radiant grin. In an instant the face was an innocent baby's face, all trace of solemn wisdom gone. I didn't know which expression I loved better.

The baby was back on my lap when we turned onto our street. My father began honking the horn the way they do at weddings, and the neighbours knew we had arrived. Betty had come over after Christopher's telephone call to tie balloons to the front of the house. Jason asked if he could carry the baby up the drive, but I told him no. I wanted to be the one to finish the journey with Sla Line. I wanted to set her down on the floor of our home and tell her she was safe at last.

There was another small ceremony I had to perform. The baby was wearing a wide plastic identification band around her ankle. In the car I had read the blue felt pen printing. SLA LINE had been hastily penned, no doubt in the last busy minutes of her stay in the refugee camp. I was anxious to remove this label, given by strangers and holding no meaning for the baby or me. Carefully, I slid the scissors under the plastic and cut the band off. It was kept and later placed with the freshly laundered blue dress, the carved wooden elephant, and Mary Jane's photos of some of the children who stayed in the refugee border camp known as Khao I Dang.

I was just removing the nameband when Betty, Jean, and Vern came in with champagne and cake and gifts. We drank a toast, made more calls, and generally spent what was left of the night drinking in the sight of this child who sat on a blanket in the middle of the room, ramrod straight, nodding her hello to everyone in turn. Fortunately I'd had the presence of mind to buy some formula at the drug store. While the baby lay back to enjoy, I decided it was time for a diaper change.

The baby was lying with the top of her head towards my father as I undid the two safety pins securing the soaked diaper. Just as I lifted back the wet cloth, my father gasped, "Oh my God, it's a boy!" My heart stopped and I almost fell forward, squashing the child, whatever it was, to death. I whipped the diaper down and saw for myself that she was, indeed, a girl. I could see how much my father was enjoying his perverse joke. He was red in the face and holding his stomach.

"You should have seen your face," he gasped. "It was priceless."

"What a very peculiar thing to say," I chastised. The boys, of course, thought it was hysterical and soon all of us fell in, though I spent the rest of the night shaking my head every time I looked at my father.

—◦—

The removal of the nameband had been a symbolic beginning. To complete the event a new name, a special one, had to be given. I had spent days reading lists from a book featuring baby names from the Third World. One in particular had struck me and I had run it by Mom. That was when the difficulty arose.

"Why give her one of those names?" she asked. "She should be named after her grandmother."

At first I thought it was a joke. But as the days wore on and more names were put forward, the same theme was played. My mother's name is Elva May, and though I love her with all my heart, I couldn't see how it would suit a Cambodian baby, who certainly would not thank me for it later. I tried a compromise. "How about May as a middle name?"

"May is not my name," my mother insisted. "Elva May is. If it can't be Elva May, then the only other thing I could understand would be if you named her after yourself. A child should be named for someone close to her."

Good Lord, she wasn't kidding. I had settled on a name I liked and it wasn't mine or my mother's. I honestly tried to warm to the idea of naming her for her grandmother, but I couldn't. Now Betty was asking me what I would call her.

"I'm not sure," I said, sliding my eyes past my mother's. We spent the rest of the night trying everyone's suggestions out. Nothing was resolved by the time our neighbours left. Still, the name I liked hadn't been tried; no one knew it. It suited the baby, as far as I was concerned. I liked the sound of it and I liked the meaning of it. LIEN (pronounced LAY-ENNE), the book stated, was said to mean "lotus flower." In Cambodia, the three large, pure petals were symbols of the country's past, present, and future, rising from the mud of the land. To me, it seemed perfect. This child symbolized her Khmer people's proud past, tragic present, and most of all their future survival. By the time we went to bed, I was already thinking of her as Lien, though I hadn't yet said it out loud.

Though we all had our own places to go home to, no one could rip themselves away and we decided to spend the night at the family house. Much the way we did at Christmas, everyone found a place to sleep. Carolyn and I claimed the room with the crib. Mom stayed with us until the baby slept. As we sat on the bed watching her struggle to keep her eyes open and fixed on me, we felt a kinship, a partnership of women so strong that though it might be stretched at times, it could never be broken.

Finally all stirring in the crib ceased. Mom stroked the small dark head of her new granddaughter before leaving. I still couldn't think of sleep. Only after more talk and watching did Carolyn suggest that we should try to rest. It was 2:00 a.m. and we had no idea of this baby's schedule or what jet lag had done to her inner time clock.

I had just drifted off when an ominous gurgle came from the direction of the crib followed by a malevolent odour. I was up, dizzy and light-headed, in a flash. In the crib, brown slime seemed to be everywhere. The baby lifted her head and smiled, unperturbed and happy to see someone close by. Even her hair was covered in muck. I tried, I really did, but when I went to lift her, she slipped through my fingers. My stomach heaved and the first gag escaped me. Then the second. Carolyn, watching languidly from the bed, long since confirmed in her ability to mother, was unsympathetic. "Honestly," she said, "it's just a little baby poop. You can't just stand there and gag every time she fills her pants. Kath, you're going to have to gear up in one awful hurry."

I tried again, and this time almost added to the mess in the crib. Carolyn rose. "Really!" she said. "Come on, Little One, your auntie will have to take care of you." Carolyn reached in and tried to lift the baby. Her big mistake was to inhale at the same time. To my utter delight she gagged, retched once, and ran for the bathroom. It was my mother who appeared, lifted the baby, bathed her, and brought her back, clean and sweet-smelling again. We changed the bed three more times that night, exhausting our supply of crib sheets.

By morning the baby, resting on towels, had sent us a very clear message. The formula we were feeding her didn't agree with her system, which was already troubled from too many months of poor conditions. The first spark of maternal concern had grown into a bonfire of worry by the time I dressed her and got her to the doctor's office in time for her appointment.

10

"THEY CAN HANDLE IT BETTER AT SICK KIDS, THAT'S ALL"

What divine intervention caused me to apply for family health insurance coverage before Sandra alerted me to the baby's arrival, I will never know. The important thing was that the waiting period was over and the baby was covered as my dependent. Now, as the doctor's receptionist tried to fill in her New Patient forms, a few unanswered questions had to be dealt with.

"The child's name?"

I looked over at my mother who was holding the baby. She raised her eyes expectantly. I remembered her saying she would understand if I named the child after myself. Feeling sick, I answered, "Lien Kathryn." My mother was silent but crestfallen, I could tell.

"Father's name?"

"I don't know," I replied.

The woman, professional that she was, accepted this bit of news with barely a lift of an eyebrow and continued with her questioning. "Birth date?"

"I don't know. There wasn't one."

This was apparently too much. "There has to have been a birth date."

"Obviously," I agreed, "but I don't know what it was."

"Well, we can't treat her without a birth date."

Again, I looked at my mother. Without any regard for school starting dates or complicated Christmases, I did the only thing I could think of to ease the blow of not naming the baby after her. "She was born on December 24, 1979." As the woman wrote that gem down, my mother sparkled and squeezed Lien a little tighter. I had to admit that it had been a bit of an inspiration, giving Lien her grandmother's birthday. The receptionist was unaware of what had just transpired, but she was happy to have the blanks filled in.

I had not yet heard Lien cry. She was content to be picked up, but was equally happy to be set down or left on her own. Going to bed was also met with blasé acceptance. She lay, examining her new surroundings and stroking the sheet beneath her, as if to absorb the feel of home. On waking, pleasant talking-to-herself noises announced that rest period was over, but there were no demands for food, diaper changes, or attention. This was a child who had never had anyone to run at her beck and call, so she took whatever came with aplomb. All of that changed once we were inside the doctor's office.

My family practitioner had always been a cool, business-like woman who had no time for nonsense from any of her patients. She never wasted time with idle chitchat and today was no different. There wasn't a trace of a smile as she eyed Lien with great objectivity and got right down to work.

"Undress her and put her on the scale," she instructed. A wrinkle formed between her eyebrows as she took note of Lien's weight. I could see that she wasn't pleased as she converted the kilos to pounds for me. "About thirteen pounds, six ounces," she muttered. Even I knew this was not a good weight for a nine-month-old infant.

On the table the baby began to look worried. She fussed a bit, looking at me and wanting to be held. By the time the examination was underway, she was screaming at full throttle. The doctor looked worried. "Has she been crying like this since she arrived?"

"No," I answered. "This is the first time. I don't know what's wrong with her."

"She sounds hungry. Is she eating well?"

"Yes," I said. "But I'm worried. I don't think I'm giving her the right thing. She has bad diarrhoea after every bottle. What if she becomes dehydrated?"

On cue, Lien soiled the table, providing more than enough of a sample for the doctor to bottle for examination.

"She can't get too bad if she's drinking formula," she said. "We'll deal with possible food allergies later. In the meantime, I need to make sure there aren't any internal parasites or diseases from the camp that might be causing the problem. For now, just feed her anything and everything she'll eat. I'll have test results soon."

We were almost finished, but then the doctor looked into the baby's ears. "Oh, my goodness," was all she said as she reached for some swabs. "No wonder she's screaming." Blackish goo covered the end of the swab as it was withdrawn. "I don't like the look of this. We'll have it cultured and call you when we know what we're dealing with. In the meantime, remember, feed her all she can take." With that, I was handed several sample cans of formula and sent on my way. I would have been more worried, except that Lien stopped crying the instant she was back in my arms and out of the office.

My mother had to agree she loved the baby's new name. We were still on a high as we bought some flowers and headed down to the Children's Aid to show her off to Sandra Scarth.

By the time we reached the Huntley Street office, Lien was sleeping. Sandra took her from me and beamed from behind moist eyes. "She's absolutely beautiful," she said. "What do you think, was she worth the wait?"

"Oh, Sandra, yes. Thank you for everything. I'm sorry I made you work so hard for this one," I said, giving her a hug. "Oh! I almost forgot. These are for you."

Sandra took the flowers from me and gave Lien back. "We've been quite a team, you and I. I'm so happy everything turned out like this. I have to admit there were days . . ."

"Never mind," I told her. "Just stick around, OK? You may not be rid of me yet. I may have my bird in the hand, but there's still . . ."

Sandra laughed — a little nervously, I thought. "I'll be here," she assured me. "I'll come round and visit the two of you at home one of these days. Take your time deciding about anything else; you've got a big adjustment to make as it is. Phone me anytime, even if it's just to let me know how you're doing."

As we left the building, Sandra called from the doorway. "Kathryn — that's one lucky little girl you've got there."

"Thanks," I said, feeling my throat tighten.

◄○►

Mom and I knew we were pressing our luck a little. Lien should have been resting at home in her own crib, but we had one last short call to make. Helen Allen was waiting for us at her apartment and we spent a quick half hour with her. We would never have heard the end of it if we hadn't. Lien continued to sleep and missed the fuss that was made over her. I left Helen's place wondering how, after being instrumental in so many placements, she could remain vitally interested in each child.

At home it was open house. We had a stream of visitors, all celebrating, all bearing gifts. Lien took each new person in stride, happy to be picked up in the middle of a rest or put down for another one. She was enjoying having people around her so much that I wondered how many long hours she had spent sitting alone in the camp. Her list of belongings was growing by leaps and bounds. By nightfall of the first day alone, she owned toys, a highchair, a Jolly Jumper, a car seat, a stroller, and a full wardrobe of dresses and sleepers. She also had a new spelling of her name.

Dad arrived home and accepted the sound of Lien, but not the way it was spelled. "People will think she's a lien on a house," he announced. "They'll say 'Leen.' They'll never give it two syllables."

Unwilling to get into the naming problem again, I compromised a little. "All right. We'll add an extra N-E at the end. That way at least they'll know enough to emphasize the second syllable." It was done. Lien was now Lienne.

On Sunday we all drove to my grandmother's cottage. She was delaying closing up until we came with the baby. There was a sense of urgency to this visit. My grandmother, at ninety-three, had not been well for months and was losing weight and finding it increasingly difficult to eat. None of us wanted to put into words our concerns, but I definitely wanted her to see this long-awaited great-grandchild now. Well or not, Grandma met the newest addition to her family tree with great acceptance and delight. She bounced Lienne on her knee, blessing her to the same Doodely, doodely, doodely, doodely, Doodely, doodely doodley-doo tune she had sung to each and every one of her grandchildren and great-grandchildren. The game seemed universal in its appeal. Lienne laughed hard from her belly, stopping only to ask with her eyes for another turn.

When we kissed the oldest member of our family goodbye the next day, I was painfully aware that our remaining visits were numbered. I didn't know then that I would never see her again.

In six weeks my grandmother, who had lived through astounding changes to the world, and who had delighted in keeping pace with them, would be gone. I know she would have told me she was only making way for the young when I wept at her funeral.

◄○►

Early on September 2, the doctor's office called and asked me to come with Lienne. The receptionist warned that I should bring a change of clothing for the baby and some extra bottles. I hurried Lienne into her new car seat and drove off. It would be ten days before either of us would be home again.

The doctor was serious when we went in. "The baby has several parasites and infections in her ears. She also has salmonella and a few other intestinal parasites. I'm sending you both down to Sick Children's Hospital now with the test results. They're expecting you. I think they are better equipped to handle all of this at once than I am. You should be prepared for them to want the baby to stay."

"That's fine," I answered, trying to quell the panic. "But if that's the case, I'm staying too. There's no way I'm leaving her there alone after all this. We're just getting to know each other."

"Tell them that. They're usually pretty good about parents bunking in, as long as they don't interfere with treatment or make a nuisance of themselves." The doctor handed me a paper with the name of the specialist who was waiting for us.

I phoned home to tell them what was happening. "Don't worry," I said, "the doctor says not one of these things is a threat if treated now. They can handle it better at Sick Kids, that's all."

As instructed, I took the baby to admitting. It didn't take long for us to run into trouble. Papers needed to be filled out. Name and birth date were no longer a problem. The Parent/Legal Guardian line was a little harder. The admitting nurse had already asked how long Lienne had been in the country and now she watched as I hesitated with the form.

"Has the child been legally adopted yet?"

"No, not yet. She will be as soon as we can manage it."

"Have you been designated her legal guardian by a court of law?"

"I think so," I hedged. "She has been placed with me."

"Do you have her Landed Immigrant status yet?"

"No," I confessed. "She just got here — I'm working on it. She has a visa, though."

"How long is it good for?"

"Thirty days, but there's no problem. Immigration is aware that she's here and will be staying. She's covered by insurance," I said, producing my card.

The nurse was kind and understood the situation, but that didn't save us. "Look, I'm asking you if you have signed a paper making you her legal guardian."

"No," I had to admit.

"Then I'm sorry. There's no way we can admit her."

"What are you saying?" I asked, knowing full well what I was up against.

"I'm saying that you are not in a position to give consent for treatment. Unless you can produce someone who is legally responsible for this child, we cannot admit her."

I was already searching for change to make a telephone call. Thankfully, Sandra Scarth was in her office. She told me not to worry, she would do something. I was to call her back in ten minutes. I fidgeted the time away, and re-dialled her number.

"I've been in touch with Mary Jane Turner. She's on her way over now. She used to be a nurse at Sick Kids. She'll be able to straighten this out, I'm sure."

Within minutes, Mary Jane arrived and went to the nurses. She didn't look happy when she returned to Lienne and me. "Just sit tight. I'll be back. If we need a guardian, that's what we'll get." In thirty minutes she had paid a call on the provincial government and was back with Attorney General Roy McMurtry in tow. He was more than happy to sign papers taking legal responsibility for the baby. He asked about her story and held Lienne for a minute. Then he wished us both good luck and signed the document.

There was a fee to cover the service and I gladly wrote a cheque for it. The paper was placed on file and the doors to the finest paediatric facility in the country were finally open to us. Mary Jane stayed long enough to see us up to the seventh floor and safely ensconced in the isolation ward. Since no one knew what, if any, vaccinations or diseases Lienne had been exposed to, this was considered best for her and the other patients. Before she left, Mary Jane promised she would come the next day to see how we were doing. The rules of the isolation unit were being explained to me when my sister arrived, wide-eyed and full of alarm. She carried a care package from home. Some of Lienne's new toys and clothing were in it. There was a sandwich for me and a few toiletries.

"We only allow parents into the ward," the nurse told us. "You have to gown up, wash your hands in the sink over there, cover your shoes with these green sacks, and leave your purse in one of the bags on the cabinet. We'll need to register the names of both parents if you and your husband intend to visit."

"I don't intend to visit," I told her. "I intend to stay."

The woman sized me up very quickly and must have decided it was no contest. She nodded her agreement. "All right, but you won't be very comfortable. The best we can offer is a chair by the cot and a blanket at night. You can stay as long as you can remain calm and get enough sleep. We don't need two patients instead of one. May I have the father's name?"

"There isn't one. But can't I put my sister down, so she can spell me off?"

"I'm sorry. We only allow mothers and fathers."

"So I'm a father," Carolyn declared. "Put me down as Charles Jackson if you like. Your book will look fine, we'll be in better shape, and Lienne will have the two people she needs to look after her."

The nurse smiled. "All right. Sign here, Dad," she said, offering the book to Carolyn.

We hadn't even seen a doctor yet, but already I felt we had made major gains. Gowned and scrubbed, we set about making the baby comfortable and happy. She didn't seem to mind where she was as long as I was with her. By now she was responding well to her name. Despite being ill, she looked noticeably chubbier and healthier than she had one short week ago.

I offered her one of the bottles we had brought with us, but before it touched her lips, the nurse was in our glass cubical to remove it. "I'm sorry," she said. "You can't give her that yet. There's a chance the doctor will want to do surgery on her ears after he sees her. There's also a very good chance he'll decide to take her off all food for twenty-four hours and then start introducing things one at a time. She'll have to wait."

Wait we did. But finally a tall, husky man swept into the ward. He was fast-moving, fast-thinking, and quite abrupt. No time for small talk here. He may have listened to the answers to his questions, but it was hard to tell. He carried Lienne into an examination room and I could hear her crying through the closed door. When the man came out, he spoke curtly to the nurse, telling her that he wanted the baby's ears irrigated twice a day for the next three days. If there wasn't enough improvement when he saw her the next time, he would perform surgery. He was the Ear, Nose, Throat specialist and I had already been told he was "the best." He wheeled out without another glance in our direction. I had read his name badge, but "Dr. God" would have suited him better.

The next team to visit was more concerned with Lienne's intestinal problems. No one could seem to comprehend that there was absolutely no medical or family history available on this child. I explained again and again that there was no possible way of tracing her parents, but was ordered to do so anyway. After much poking and prodding, the decision was made: no food or formula for the next twenty-four hours. Then Lienne could start with mashed bananas. Rice would follow if all went well.

A small Chinese medical student lingered after the others left. Her English was very limited, which may have accounted for the fact that she missed hearing where Lienne had come from.

"She Chinese?" the girl asked, looking very serious and thoughtful.

"No," I answered. "She's Cambodian."

"Ah! Good. 'Cause if she Chinese, she retarded." Having made this pronouncement, the tiny sage disappeared from our presence, secure in the knowledge that the wide-set eyes of my daughter didn't signal further trouble.

Lienne did not like water. She was addicted to the plentiful food and all those unlimited bottles she had come to expect in the last week. In very short order she had the haunted look of someone suffering from withdrawal. I didn't like denying her what she wanted, especially after promising her she would never be hungry again. Carolyn and I sang and played and invented every baby game we could come up with until the wee hours of the morning, when the poor thing finally gave up waiting and drifted off to sleep.

By morning, Lienne was something of a celebrity. Nurses were spreading the word and many were dropping by to offer encouragement and assurances. She was soon dubbed "Punkin," a name I'm certain many babies go by at the hospital. One kind nurse's eyes welled with tears when she heard Lienne's history. "Oh, poor little thing. Do you think she understands what we're saying?"

"I don't think so," I replied. "But she does seem to know her new name."

"Well," the nurse offered helpfully, "we'll just have to get an interpreter up here."

I was baffled. "What good do you think that would do? What, besides goo-goo, do you think she would tell us?"

The woman looked startled, then burst into embarrassed laughter. "Of course," she blushed. "I was so concerned I forgot she can't speak in any language!" She left the ward still laughing at herself.

We had many more visitors that day, but we did not see the people we needed to see. No one had appeared the night before or that morning to flush out Lienne's ears. She was increasingly hungry and irritable. I began to make inquiries on a regular basis, every time the nurses came within speaking distance. The answer was always the same. The resident on duty was busy with emergencies. He had been paged, but hadn't shown. There was nothing they could do. Finally, I left the room, went through the de-gowning process, and entered the contaminated atmosphere of the corridor. Information from the nursing station confirmed that the doctor was unavailable. He would show up as soon as they could get hold of him. Lienne and I were both miserable by the time Carolyn came from work to relieve the monotony.

So far we had nothing to show for our first day except diapers empty of anything but urine. This was a good start, but I had heard what the doctor had said about the ears. Surgery wasn't high on my wish list. Even though Carolyn complained before going home to Christopher, no one came. I sat up all night waiting, but by morning nothing had happened. All the next day I repeatedly de-gowned, inquired at the nursing station, scrubbed, gowned again, and waited some more. Nothing.

We did take one small step forward: Lienne was finally offered something more or less solid to eat. A small jar of mashed bananas accompanied the bottle of distilled water for breakfast. The poor baby gobbled every bit of it and looked anxious for more. More arrived at noon. This jar was eaten only slightly less eagerly. By dinner, Lienne ate as though it was her job, and by eleven, I had to coax more than a little to get her to finish the bananas. Still, no one arrived to look after her ears.

Wild with worry, I kept haranguing the nurses. They bore it all with patient grace and agreed it was terrible. But they had done everything they could and the doctor was well aware that we were waiting. All we could do was wait some more.

Time began to run together. Carolyn was with me again, singing "I'm Chiquita Banana" to Lienne who refused to look at another spoonful of the muck we were offering. Finally, the spoon wafted a little too close to her nose and she gagged. The nurse was watching.

"That does it," she said. "Enough bananas, already. I'll order some rice and we'll see how that sits. Poor little Punkin."

The rice was a huge hit. Every grain was gone and wonder of wonders, nothing happened as a result. Lienne has never been able to stand the smell of bananas, let alone eat one, to this day.

Late that night, as Carolyn and I watched the nurses caring for babies far more fragile than Lienne, my mother arrived. She tapped on the glass windows from the small change room where the gowns were kept. I got up and walked stiffly over to the window. Mom had pressed a cable up to the glass.

Kathie, why are you not answering your phone? Imperative that you send the name you will give Mari in order to complete papers. Attny. states you must attend adoption hearing in Manila. Courts becoming more strict. Send name immediately. We must proceed quickly.

Emilia

I looked past the paper and into my mother's eyes. I had been dreading this. After only days with a sick baby, there was no more time to decide later. Bone weary and sick with worry, I was close to tears. It was unfair to have to decide like this, while everything with Lienne was still so unsettled and new. I experienced a pang of guilt along with the realization that I no longer felt the same urgency to have Mari. I had my child and I was totally happy with her. Why, after all this, couldn't I just enjoy everything? Mom could read my mind. She signalled me to come out and talk to her.

"How are you holding up?" she asked, noting the dark circles under my eyes.

"All right, I guess. Lienne's OK, but nothing's happened with her ears. I'm ready to scream the walls down, but then I'll get kicked out for being hysterical. Mom, what am I going to do? I can't think anymore."

"You're going to give me the name to send to Emilia, that's what. You know you aren't going to forget about that child now. Why agonize over the decision and make yourself sick?"

I started to cry. "Because, what if I can't handle two kids? Lesley said I'd be wiped off the map. I'm not that great right now after seven days with one baby."

"Well, I don't know Lesley all that well, but I do know you. You'll handle whatever you want. Once Lienne is healthy and you've had some sleep, things will be different."

"If I go ahead, I'm going to need lots of help. Are you prepared to look after both kids while I'm at work?"

"Sure. I was ready for one. Your father is retiring soon and he'll be around. The boys are big enough to be really helpful and your sister lives five blocks away. It's not such a big deal. We're talking about two children, not twenty. You feed one, you feed two. You change two diapers instead of one. So what? You can do it and so can I. You'll have help if you need it."

The tears were streaming now. "But, Mom," I choked. "If I send a name, I'm going to go and get her. You know that, don't you?"

"Just give me the name and get it over with."

"Good grief," I snuffled, "do I have to call this one Elva May?"

We both started laughing. "No. I wouldn't do that to my worst enemy. Call her whatever you like."

Carolyn was standing at the window watching from the germfree side. I held the telegram up to her and her hand flew to her mouth. We all ended up laughing like three idiots. I took a slip of paper from my purse and wrote MIGUELA CAROLYN on it and handed it to my mother. "Cable her when you get home," I told her.

"Hmph. Nice name," she said. "Where the hell did it come from?"

"From *The Third World Baby Name Book*, where else? It's Spanish, but it's used a lot in the Philippines. It's the female form of Michael, meaning like unto God."

"Well," said my mother, "I guess that's better than Elva May, meaning sprightly wood nymph."

We broke the rules that night. The isolation ward had a visit from a grandmother, properly scrubbed and covered. My mother was upset at the bruises on Lienne's hand, reminders of the intravenous tubes that had been in place until that afternoon, when the rice had been eaten and tolerated without difficulty. At least progress was being made in that area.

Later, after Carolyn and Mom had left, the nurse came over and told me she had shoved one of the leather waiting room lounge chairs into an empty storage room. "I've put a blanket and pillow and a couple of towels in there. Why don't you go and lie down for a while? I'll be here all night and you can be back before the baby wakes up in the morning."

I looked over at my sleeping child. It was 1:00 a.m. Nothing more would happen tonight. "Thanks," I said, picking myself up. Within minutes I was asleep in my own private room.

—◄o►—

My eyes flew open and I fumbled for the light switch. In this windowless chamber it was impossible to get a sense of time. To my relief, my wristwatch showed 6:30. I hurried to get dressed and be back with Lienne by the time she was awake. Still groggy, I arrived to find her sitting straight in her bed, happily eating more rice. The nurse handed me the spoon as I sat down beside her.

At 7:45, the door swung open and in came Dr. God and entourage. He set about examining Lienne immediately and, not surprisingly, was unhappy with her progress.

"That's because she hasn't had any treatment," I ventured.

"Nonsense!" he said. "I'll do surgery later this afternoon."

"Excuse me, but you won't," I replied.

The doctor glared at me in silence for quite some time. Nurses, interns, and students froze. "And who might you be?" he finally asked.

"I'm her mother. We met three days ago. There hasn't been anyone in to look at her ears since you left. I won't agree to surgery until she's had a chance to improve."

This was not a man to be told what would or would not happen. "Don't be ridiculous," he shouted. "Of course she's had the treatment. I ordered it!"

I stood my ground. "Look on the chart. You may have ordered it, but it hasn't happened."

"It most certainly has," the man fumed, full of righteous indignation. "It simply was done when you weren't here, that's all."

I could feel my self-control slipping badly. "It has not been done — not even once. I have been here the whole time. I've been going crazy bothering everyone on this floor. The doctor has been paged steadily since you left, but he hasn't come. If you don't believe me, why won't you look at the chart, you pompous ass!"

The doctor in front of me was turning purple. Eyes all around us lowered. "Well, I guess you didn't make a big enough fuss, did you?" he sneered.

That tore it. Sleep deprivation and stress won out. My hands flew up to the lapels of his white lab coat. I pulled him forward until he was very close to my face. "What did you say?" I whispered in my most sinister tone.

"I said, if you are her mother, I guess you didn't make a big enough fuss to get anything accomplished. And furthermore, if you expect me to take you seriously, you had better take your hands off me!" The doctor was uncurling my fingers one by one.

I was more than happy to relinquish my grip, but not the argument.

"You're obviously comfortable being the Big Cheese around here. It's your damn job to give the orders AND see that they're followed. You make the fuss, go on! You get something done. Then if it doesn't work, we'll talk about surgery."

The morning nurse, calm only moments before, was suddenly very flustered. She stepped between us. "I'm sorry, doctor, it's true. We've all been trying to contact the resident. Look, she's correct. There has been no treatment."

The chart was shoved under the doctor's nose. He looked at it long enough to register there was nothing on it. In a rage, he wheeled, hollering the unfortunate resident's name all the way to the nursing station at the end of the hall. I picked up Lienne who had been frightened by all the noise. Uncertain of what to do, the students on morning rounds began to shuffle out one by one.

I was certain I no longer qualified as calm or unobtrusive. I stood miserably, waiting to be ordered out. Instead, the remaining nurse turned to me and beamed.

"Well done, my dear!" she praised in her warm Jamaican accent. "Now, why don't you go and get yourself a nice, hot morning coffee? You deserve it, and that's for true!"

11

"WHAT TIME DID SHE EAT LAST?"

Lienne's treatment began ten minutes later and from the first session, her days on the isolation ward were numbered. Her skin became silky and soft, and her hair lost its dry, reddish cast and began to take on a sheen. Arms and legs were becoming round and firm and muscular. We all took a special delight in each ounce gained. I wasn't at all surprised when, three days later, the specialist arrived and declared "magnificent progress." He studiously avoided glancing in my direction and neither of us mentioned our earlier incident. He instructed his students carefully, and told them to take special note of this child. "She is a beautifully proportioned infant," he remarked, giving Lienne an approving, kindly look.

Despite my dislike for this man, my heart swelled with pride. I was thrilled at my baby's escape from his knife and vindicated in my determination to resist the surgery. Before leaving, the doctor ordered ongoing care, which was delivered religiously and on time to the minute.

Eleven days after our entry, Lienne was finally declared more or less fit. Though she still showed signs of salmonella in her stool, all the parasites had abandoned ship. She was able to eat and retain her food long enough to receive sustenance from it. Her milk diet had been replaced with a soya formula because of an intolerance for lactose. Her ears were free of infection and mites and her specialist was mightily pleased when he paid his last visit and signed her release. He did comment, in my general direction, that there was a strong likelihood Lienne would suffer recurring bouts of ear infection, since this was now a weak spot for her. We were told to turn up at his clinic in six weeks for hearing tests and a check-up. The doctor was not unfriendly on this occasion, and my opinion of him was somewhat softened as I watched him say goodbye to my little girl.

I was close to tears as we parted with the nurses who had so carefully looked after Lienne. I was reluctant as well to leave the other babies in the unit without knowing their outcome. In very short order we had become a little community. Once downstairs, however, I was full of eagerness to be home again. I paid the required visit to the accounts office on the main floor and was shocked at the sum of Lienne's bill. My lucky stars had indeed been shining on the day I chose to apply for family coverage.

We had almost made it, until it came time to sign the release form. Somehow the guardianship paper was not in the file where it belonged. The question of who was responsible for Lienne came up again.

"I'm sorry, but you cannot remove the baby from the hospital until we have another signed document for the file," I was told.

I'd had enough. Hoisting Lienne and her diaper bag a little higher, I made it very clear we were leaving. "You know as well as I do that that paper was on file when we were admitted. If it isn't there now, it's not my problem. I am taking the baby home this minute. You have my address and phone number. Call me if you need any more information." With that, Lienne and I headed into the bright sunshine of a September day and settled back home where we belonged. We were never reprimanded about our improper exit.

—◄○►—

I had only planned on being away from the office for two weeks, but Lienne's stay in the hospital changed that a little. She was released early on a Friday. Even with the weekend we still hadn't had enough time to adjust to home or a routine. I decided to spend another three of my carefully hoarded vacation days. By Thursday I returned to the office, reluctant to leave the baby, but eager to prove I was sharp and competent, even if my world no longer revolved around my job alone. I worked hard to concentrate, but missed Lienne terribly. The first day was the hardest, but I managed to do it with only one lunchtime phone call to Mom. Still, as I waited for the last of my staff to leave that afternoon, I counted the minutes till I could be home.

Everything was in order when I got there, and Lienne was happy to see me. We had just begun the pattern that would be our normal one for the next few years to come. Gradually, we got Lienne into the habit of two quite long sleeps during the day, so that by the time I was back from work, she was good until 10:30 or 11:00 p.m. We had plenty of time for walks and play and visits with friends.

Because my job had to be important if I was going to go on supporting this child and possibly a second one, I developed a simple way of turning my thoughts of home off and on while travelling to and from work. I chose a landmark, my favourite tree, and as soon as I passed it on my way north, I made a conscious effort to stop thinking of Lienne and start thinking of work. Coming south in the evenings, after passing the tree, I would put all business of the day behind me and start thinking of the baby. The "switch-around tree" performed an immense service for me, especially whenever I heard from Emilia and remembered she was working to prepare Mari's papers.

For a while I was full of energy and relieved to find that looking after a baby and an art department was far easier than thinking about it for months on end. Even Lesley was calmer now, as she began to see I wasn't going to be "wiped off the map."

Life was perfect — until the superintendent arrived to let the air out of the radiators in preparation for winter. He noticed the high chair in the dining room and he most certainly noticed the crib, complete with sleeping infant in the small bedroom. Nevertheless, he completed his mission and left without comment. Three days later, I was in receipt of a registered letter informing me that I was living in an "adult only" building, had not asked permission to have a child, and would be leaving in three months' time. I was to make my suite ready for prospective tenants to come through the following week.

My heart sank. It's true there were no other children in the building, yet I remembered going to school with kids who had lived in it. I had always assumed the absence of children reflected a preference for renting to childless couples or single people. Now here I was with one new child, facing eviction while making plans to adopt a second baby.

A few inquiries turned up some interesting information. The four-storey, low-rise building had never been designated adult only. Children had, in fact, lived there, the superintendent's son being one of them. As long as my child didn't cause complaints and disrupt the other tenants, it appeared we were within our rights to stay.

One call to a legal office confirmed the information. The lawyer I had chosen, well known for defending women's rights, certainly didn't sound like she would accept any nonsense. I asked her to write a letter to the management of our building.

"Don't be silly. You don't need a letter from me or anyone else. Just make sure the baby isn't bothering anyone. How are your neighbours about this?"

"They're fine, I guess. I never see them and, to tell the truth, they probably don't even know there's a baby in here. The woman to my right is in her eighties and deaf. The two sisters below me are elderly and hard of hearing, too. We're on the top floor on a corner of the building, so there is no neighbour to the left."

"Perfect," the lawyer said. "I advise you to get the neighbour to your right onside so she isn't likely to complain. Then just keep your door locked and don't let them show anyone through your suite."

"I can't keep them out while I'm at work," I reasoned. "I would really appreciate a letter from you. If they're bluffing, it might be enough to stop them from bothering me. I'm going to the Philippines shortly to bring back another child. I haven't got the time, energy, or money to move. I don't even want to argue with these people."

"I'll do the letter if you want, but I strongly urge you to woo the support of your neighbour. They may try to use her if they are serious about getting rid of you."

Late that evening I did happen to see Mrs. Graham on my way to the incinerator. She had always been pleasant enough with me, but had a reputation of being a complainer with many of the other residents. I decided I had to take a chance on her.

"Hello, Mrs. Graham," I said. "How have you been?"

"What? Fine, dear, but you are looking tired. I haven't seen you for a long time. Have you been unwell?"

"Oh, no," I told her, turning up my volume so she could hear. "I have been busy, though. I hope you haven't been bothered by the noise."

"What noise, dear? I never hear a peep from you."

"Then you haven't noticed anything lately?" I asked again, trying to get her to commit before I spilled the beans.

"Not a thing," she said. "Why?"

"I'd like to show you why," I said, inviting her into my place. Lienne was asleep in her crib, looking very peaceful and very quiet. Mrs. Graham was immediately taken with her and listened to the whole story, enthralled. Between the two of us, we managed to wake Lienne, who thankfully raised her head with a smile on her face, looking like the most pleasant baby in the world. I picked her up and carried her to the living room, handing her to Mrs. Graham so I could make some tea. She was definitely onside when she left that night.

"Don't you worry about a thing, dear," she said as she opened the door. "If they try to kick you out, we'll go to the newspapers with it. They won't want that embarrassment."

I thanked my newest ally and rested more easily that night. The fact that baby number two was a real possibility and hadn't been mentioned yet was only slightly unsettling.

The lawyer did send a letter. It outlined how I had always been a good tenant, had paid my rent on time, did not constitute a nuisance, and intended to carry on in such a manner. Management was warned that undue harassment would lead to follow-up from her office. The letter hit its target and was well worth the money. I never heard another word from anyone about leaving. For the moment, Lienne and I were safe. What might happen if Mari came I would have to deal with later.

◄○►

By the end of my second week back at the office, I had found my rhythm. Fatigue was masked by happiness. I was managing my responsibilities at work and keeping up with the laundry and other work at home. Best of all, I had plenty of time for Lienne.

Weekends were the best. I was looking forward to another one on a Friday afternoon when the office phone rang.

"Miss Cole? It's Vera Small in Barbados. I have wonderful news! We have a beautiful six-month-old girl here who is ready to travel to Canada. There will be no trouble this time. She has been examined by your friend and as soon as you tell us, we can proceed with her papers."

"Will the baby find a good home if I cannot take her?" I asked without a moment's hesitation.

"Yes, I suppose . . ."

"That's wonderful," I cut in. "Because I have just received a baby from Cambodia. Not only that, I'm going to Manila to adopt a second little girl as soon as a court date is assigned. I really think that three children under the age of two would be more than I could handle. I'm sorry. I didn't expect to hear back from you after such a long time. I should have let you know, but in the rush of everything that was happening here, I didn't think to call you."

Vera understood and agreed that babies in bunches were generally to be avoided. She congratulated me on Lienne and wished me luck with Mari before hanging up. Lesley had been sitting in my office the whole time. She smiled as I replaced the receiver. "Thank goodness you did that," she said with a wry smile. "I didn't think you had it in you."

That Saturday Lienne and I had a wonderful day. She was awake at her usual 7:00 a.m., babbling happily in her crib. Once I felt I had enjoyed lying in bed long enough, I rose and warmed a bottle of greyish soya formula. While she slept that morning, I did laundry and ironed, anxious for her to wake up so we could go out for a walk.

Down in the park Lienne examined and crunched colourful fall leaves between her fingers. We were out for the best part of the day. Back at home, there was another short nap and another play period. Then things began to deteriorate. Lienne never woke up cranky, but this time she did. I went in to her room and she stopped complaining only long enough to be changed. Unconcerned at first, I tried to jolly her out of the bad mood. An hour later I was taking her temperature. It was normal. I checked her ears. No telltale sign of any discharge. Her top two teeth had cut through nicely and there didn't seem to be a sign of any other teething activity. Still, with each half hour that passed Lienne got more and more worked up. I tried Gripe Water and Carolyn's trusty mixture of ground ginger and sugar water, in case gas pains were the source of the trouble. Lienne tossed her head and spat out what little had managed to find its way into her mouth. Finally, around 7:00 p.m., I gave in to my alarm and called Carolyn.

"Can you come over?" I asked. "Something's wrong with Lienne. I can't get her to stop crying. She must be sick."

Even her aunt's arrival didn't cheer Lienne up. She was ruddy from crying and couldn't have cared less who was there. Carolyn took one look at her and said, "What time did she eat last?"

The question struck like a slap in the face. Carolyn had already noticed my look of shock so there was no point in trying to cover up.

"Well, when did she eat last?"

"Oh, Carolyn! The only thing she's had today was her morning bottle. We were having such a good time, I totally forgot to feed her!"

"My God, Kath!" my sister yelled as she snatched Lienne up and rushed into the kitchen. "I told you before! You are going to have to gear up if you're going to do this."

I burst into tears, full of remorse and indignation. "What do you mean, *if* I'm going to do it? I *am* doing it. I forgot, that's all. I know babies eat, for heaven's sake."

Lienne was silent for the first time in a while. But even as she packed away her dinner, her body shuddered with dry sobs. I couldn't have felt more stupid, or less useful, as my sister spooned food into her open mouth. I sat, silent, until Carolyn finally took pity on me.

"I'm sorry," she said. "I was just surprised, that's all."

"Me too," I admitted. "I never forgot to feed her before. Promise you won't tell anybody."

We laughed. "That might be too much to ask," Carolyn warned. "I'm going to go back to get Chris. The two of us will stay over tonight so you can go to bed early and sleep in tomorrow."

That one long night's sleep was all I needed. By morning I was back on track and doing fine.

◄o►

Six weeks after Lienne's release from the hospital, we were on our way to the clinic for her examination and hearing tests. Lienne was now a very different-looking child. She was robust and standing quite steadily on her own. Dressed in her prettiest clothes and wearing her new walking shoes, she was the picture of good health.

The picture wasn't lost on her doctor. He was visibly surprised and obviously pleased when he saw her. After looking into Lienne's ears, and doing a few simple tests, he turned and spoke directly to me for the first time since our confrontation in the hospital.

"I guess I owe you an apology," he said.

"I guess you do," I agreed, trying not to look surprised.

The doctor hesitated. "It's just that I see so many cases of abuse and neglect in this job. I was very upset at the condition this baby was in. Her head was literally a sewer."

"That may be," I rejoined. "But you wouldn't read the chart. Surely you could see the baby didn't look much like me and there might be a story behind us. I can even understand your anger with me, but you were willing to let Lienne pay the price by not being sure of her treatment."

The doctor flushed red, a sure sign that we were on the brink again. His voice was gruff. "I said I was sorry, didn't I?"

I smiled ruefully. "You know, I don't believe you quite managed that yet."

"Well, I'm sorry."

"It's all right."

"Good." The doctor smiled and held out his hand. We shook and our truce was formed. It was a good thing too. Throughout Lienne's first winter, the doctor's prediction of recurring otitis media would come true. We visited him more times than I cared to count. In the coming years, we would be referred to him over and over again by other doctors who considered him "the best."

For a while we had yet another new person in our lives, but he wasn't exactly welcomed by all of us. He turned up late one afternoon as I was preparing dinner. I opened the door to a short, dour-looking man who seemed to have very little to say for himself. In low tones he told me he was from the Department of Health. There had been a report of salmonella in our home and he had come to inspect.

"There isn't much to inspect," I told him. "The salmonella didn't originate here. My baby came from overseas with it."

But Mr. McMann had a job to do whatever the source of the trouble. He looked around the apartment and filled out a report as he sat on the couch. Then, reaching into his brown paper bag, he produced one canister for Lienne and one for everyone who had been in close contact with her. Seven sample canisters were lined up neatly with firm instructions that every family member, from my father on down, should provide a stool sample, and fill, mix, and mail the kits at the first opportunity. I was dubious as to how this request would be received by the rest of my family.

The first round of canisters was accepted with a few suspicious looks but with equanimity. We all performed in due time and dropped the canisters in the mailbox. I never gave it another thought until the following week, when peering through my apartment door peephole, I spied Mr. McMann, looking extremely depressed as he stood with yet another brown bag in hand.

"Mr. McMann," I said. "You're back."

"Yes. All the tests were negative except for Lienne's. Everyone will have to provide more samples until they are all negative." Seven more empty canisters were deposited and the unhappy Mr. McMann left.

Again, we all obliged, though there were serious complaints this time. The third and fourth week brought more visits from Mr. McMann. Finally, there was out-and-out rebellion. No one was willing to use one more popsicle stick or mix one more vile-smelling concoction of chemicals and faeces.

The last time I opened the door to Mr. McMann, I could have recited his spiel. "Let me guess," I said. "The baby's test is still positive, everyone else's is negative."

"That is correct," he said self-importantly. He was already counting out seven more canisters when I stopped him.

"Look," I reasoned. "I'm willing to go on sending Lienne's samples and mine for as long as you like. But I can no longer promise the cooperation of everyone else in the family. They refuse to participate any further."

Mr. McMann immediately began putting all of his canisters back into the bag. "All right," he said in his expressionless mono- tone. "These things have a way of looking after themselves anyway, if you know what I mean."

I had fully expected Mr. McMann to threaten us with a higher authority. "No, I don't know what you mean," I said.

"Well, with salmonella, you can pretty well count on it to run its course. It will go away eventually. Just be careful to wash your hands after changing the baby and promise me you won't play in her diaper, if you know what I mean."

I was suddenly consumed with curiosity to know what Mr.

McMann did for recreation at home, but I didn't even consider asking. Instead, I promised easily that I would stay away from the contents of each and every diaper I might be tempted to play in. "Can you just clarify something for me?" I asked as he rose to leave. "Do you mean I could have refused to do this from the very outset?"

"You could say that, I guess," he admitted, placing his dull brown hat on his head.

Instead of throttling him with his brown paper bag, I somehow managed to hold open the door, and the intrepid little defender of our public health left — never to return again.

◄◦►

Clear of medical problems and apparently written off by the Department of Health, we were free to enjoy the best Christmas yet. Lienne took her first solo steps two days before her birthday. She waited until I got home, so I didn't miss seeing this important milestone. On Christmas Eve she was resplendent in the new dress her grandmother had sewn for her birthday. To me, there had never been, nor could there be, a more exquisite child. The fact that she was mine was nothing short of miraculous. We had a party to remember that first year. Open house went on into the small hours of the morning, keeping Santa's official visit at bay. But when he did come, he left something special for all the children, including Mari.

She was not to be forgotten. The excitement of Christmas Eve was heightened not only by the first dual birthday party, but also by the news I had received that week. The court date had been set in Manila. Mari's adoption hearing was officially scheduled for January 27. Carolyn had promised to come with me and she was as good as her word. We had purchased our airline tickets and had a departure date of January 22.

The only sadness came from the fact that for the first time in her life, my mother did not hear the story of what a very precious Christmas gift she had been. My grandmother had died in October, but the bond between Christmas babies and their mothers is everlasting. I discovered my mother alone and weeping more than once that night, her grief mixing with our Christmas joy.

12

MY EYES BEGAN SEARCHING
FOR . . . MARI

In the flurry of preparing to leave for Manila, I had to think of much more than what to pack, although that was definitely a problem. All autumn, I had been working to get Lienne through the various stages of paperwork so that eventually I could apply for her Canadian citizenship. At this point, Lienne's emergency Red Cross visa had been extended and we were waiting for an immigrant visa. At the same time, I was expecting a new Order of Guardianship from the Ministry of the Attorney General, making me Lienne's official guardian. Now I was working again with Employment and Immigration Canada, but this time in preparation for Mari.

The office had closed over Christmas and the break had done me good. After the New Year, I was back and working at double speed, partly because I was so excited and partly because I wanted everything well organized before taking more holiday time. The managing director wasn't in the least concerned when

I told him about baby number two. He simply smiled.

"I guess I'll have to get used to this," he said. "I have a feeling this child is just the second of many."

"You're wrong," I stated firmly. "Trust me, after this, I'm finished."

My kind boss chuckled. "That may be what you think now, but we'll see, won't we?"

I didn't want to disillusion anyone who thought I was on a par with Mother Theresa, so I didn't prove my point by telling him I had already turned down a third child. Besides, I was grateful to have his unconditional support.

On the advice of the Employment and Immigration officials, I had written twice to the Immigration Section of the Canadian Embassy in Manila, letting them know of my plans to adopt, and giving them our arrival and departure dates. The stage had been set and everything seemed quite straightforward.

Carolyn and I had both gone to our family doctor and had the required shots and immunizations. She gave us cholera and typhoid vaccines, but she decided anti-malaria medication was unnecessary when we told her we wouldn't be in the countryside.

Things were more or less on an even keel. All was still quiet on the eviction front. Lienne's health was restored and work was fine. Not only that, Mother had been absolutely correct. I wanted Mari now, as much as I had before. In fact, I wanted her so much that I decided not to tell anyone in the Philippines, least of all Emilia Sanches, about Lienne. There was no point in taking the urgency or polish off the work she was doing at her end. In this, I was dishonest with my friend in Manila for the first time.

As for packing, there was much to consider. My finances were beginning to show some strain. The airfare to Manila was not cheap, Christmas had taken its toll, expenses for Lienne had run high, and I had to ensure that I still had the money to give Emilia for legal fees and expenses. She had advised me to bring $3,700 to cover everything. I had the money, but not much more than that as I went shopping for gifts for Emilia's family, as well as for the perfect outfit to wear to court.

It took three forays to make the final choice. Whatever I wore had to give me an air of "controlled affluence," thus ensuring the judge that I was wealthy enough to be responsible financially, even if I was single. However, I didn't want to look like I was someone who would raise the child at arm's length, handing her over to a string of nannies and servants. I had to look professional enough to be taken seriously, but I had to avoid being crisp and cold at all costs. I needed to seem mature but definitely not over the hill; fashionable but not trendy; feminine but not fluffy.

In the middle of one dressing room Carolyn baldly stated that I was becoming a mental case about this outfit. At that point, I chose an expensive off-white, raw silk suit with a long-sleeved rose-coloured blouse. The skirt had a deep slit up the side, which, I'm ashamed to admit, I hoped would be facing the judge's chair. It was quite elegant and fit like a dream. I forgot to consider the heat and humidity of Manila in January as I paid for it, bought shoes and stockings to match, and went home flushed with success.

The rest of my wardrobe was a disaster. Mom offered what she had in her cupboard and presented me with a cute little number she had purchased on sale. It was a loose-fitting, "comfortable" dress with quite ridiculous layers of ruffles around the bottom. The print was pretty, but the material was hideous. It was the sort of nylon one finds in nightgowns. In truth, I was uncertain if this garment was meant to be day or night wear. Not wanting to offend, I accepted the dress with all the right words of thanks and appreciation and jammed it into the already full bag.

Good jewellery was left behind; I never travel with it. I did include a fake gold chain and a pin, hoping a little glitter might dress up the suit and disguise the flouncy nightgown. The last thing I placed in the bag was the first thing I hoped to remove from it. The little plush penguin, wrapped in tissue paper, was for Mari.

On January 21, my co-workers wished me all the best and sent me off with a party. As of the first of January, I was entitled to four more weeks of paid vacation. If I took three weeks in a chunk — two for travelling, and the third pathetically short one to get to know Mari and settle her into a routine — I'd be back by February 12. Of course, I wouldn't need the third week if we returned empty-handed. My plan left one precious week for emergencies or maybe even a holiday later in the year.

My parents were a little upset. They had planned a trip to Florida before knowing what the court date would be and they wavered on the brink of cancelling their plans when we found out that the two dates conflicted. In the end, Carolyn and I convinced them to go. They would need to be well rested if Mari returned with us.

It was my aunt who stepped in and saved the situation. My grandmother had always lived with her in Ottawa and now Aunt Phyllis was not only lonely, but also free to come and look after Lienne and the boys. This was the very aunt whose baby I had watched over all those years ago. She owed me one — big time.

Aunt Phyllis arrived a week before our departure and got to know Lienne and her routine before any of us disappeared. There was no one I would have felt more comfortable leaving the baby with. The only worry I had was that Lienne would forget who I was, or prefer Aunt Phyllis by the time I got back.

I sat in the rocker by Lienne's crib the night before we left, watching her drift off to sleep. That night we spent our last moments as a twosome. She lay, as she always did, on her stomach, feeling the sheet with her long fingers. This tiny ritual was always the sign that sleep was imminent. I rose and stroked her back, whispering how much I would miss her. I promised to

117

try to bring her back a sister and promised, too, that I would always love her.

This was one of those occasions that called for intense rationalization and I indulged wholeheartedly that night. The depth of my relationship with Lienne was wonderful and perfect for now. But we really were a single parent and an only child, with nothing to focus on except each other. Surely this would be crippling for one of us eventually. Yes, a mother with two children was more of a family unit. And both of the girls would have someone beyond me to rely upon. They would have each other long after they were grown, just as I had my sister.

-◄o►-

Carolyn and I were in a high state of excitement before climbing into the airport limousine the next day. I kissed each member of the family, and squeezed Lienne tight. My mother and aunt stood side by side and I tried to swallow the lump in my throat as I handed Lienne over to them.

"Bring us another baby," were my father's last words as he closed the door behind us.

Once on the plane, we settled ourselves in for the long journey. Fortunately Malaya Mendoza, tickled pink that her offer of help had resulted in our trip, had provided us with all sorts of reading material. She had also promised to inform her father that we were on the way, so that he could monitor our progress through the courts. It appeared we could have legal backup if necessary.

Our route took us through Chicago and we spent the night with some friends. Tony and Kaye were excited about our mission and we talked for hours about all the possibilities and pitfalls we might face. They promised to be at the airport when we came through again on our homeward journey. We would have two hours between flights and they wanted to be there to see Mari-Miguela if she was with us.

Before we knew it, we were on the long leg of the trip, flying towards Tokyo, where we would change planes for Manila. With a twelve-hour time change and many more hours of flying ahead of us, I was having trouble keeping track of the date.

By the time we reached Tokyo, Carolyn and I were on automatic pilot. We had tried to sleep on the plane, but it was no use: we were too excited. Now, rumpled and bleary-eyed, we sat waiting for our boarding call, wondering about so many things.

I was curious to meet Emilia after so many letters and phone conversations. She was an enigma, despite our many contacts. I had no idea of what she looked like. Carolyn and I discussed all the possibilities surrounding the court case, and, given those uncertainties, I was resolved not to become too involved with the baby until she was declared mine. We spoke of Lienne and how much we already missed her, but mostly we wondered about Mari. I was a few short hours away from seeing her in the flesh and assumed this occasion would be as joyful as the first.

"Do you think Emilia will have the baby at the airport to meet us?" I asked.

"I don't know. Maybe," Carolyn mused. "But don't be disappointed if she doesn't. She'll likely think it's best to leave her at home. It'll be around 10:30 at night there when we land. Mari will probably be in bed."

Carolyn was no doubt right, but even so, I imagined for a moment that I was Emilia. If I was meeting someone who had come from the other side of the world to adopt a baby, I would have the child with me.

We fell silent as the plane approached the runway. At this point, we had been en route for almost thirty-six hours.

All sensation of fatigue had vanished by the time we stepped with swollen feet into the baggage claim area. The air terminal was crowded and bustling, even though the luggage conveyer belts had not yet started up. I glanced into the crowd waiting behind a railing about twenty-five feet away. There, slightly to the left, stood a woman holding a cardboard sign with my name on it. She was grinning broadly and accompanied by two young girls. Then I looked down.

Directly in front of Emilia, with its back to us, stood a tiny little thing, dressed in a blue pantsuit.

"Look! There she is!" I told my sister as I picked up speed and walked towards the group of people. Emilia waved in recognition, but I barely returned her smile as I reached down to the narrow shoulders of the child I had waited so long to see.

The second my hands made contact, the blue-suited figure wheeled to face me. To my horror I was bending over the upturned face of a very homely male midget who was somewhere in his mid-fifties. As the acne-scarred skin, receding hairline, hooked nose, and sharp, hawk-like eyes registered, I sucked in air.

It's hard to know which of us was more startled, but the midget recovered first. Pointing his finger up at me, he ordered in strident tones for one so small, "Get your bag! Get your bag!" He should have run for his life; a giantess in shock was about to crash like a felled oak.

While I struggled to stay upright and to exhale, Emilia chimed in, "Welcome, Kathie. Yes, yes, hurry! Get your bags."

I staggered back to the conveyer belt, which by now had swung into motion. Carolyn, having witnessed my debacle, had caught up and was trying to speak. I immediately veered away from her, hissing, "Get away. Stand somewhere else!"

The tiny man had attached himself to me and demanded to know which of the hundreds of bags was mine. It was hard to tell; I couldn't see past the water in my eyes. Impatiently, he jumped up on the moving track and began leaping from suitcase to suitcase rather like a monkey. "Is it this? No? This?" he demanded, as he whizzed back and forth. Finally, he cartwheeled close to my drab, olive green suitcase.

"That one," I managed to say, and he jumped on top of it and sat cross-legged. This must have been a pre-arranged signal. A pair of long, muscular arms reached from behind me and lifted both the bag and the little man onto a luggage cart. In a flash, the midget jumped off and repeated the whole amazing procedure in search of Carolyn's bag. This time I had the pleasure of observing her, as she stood watching the bizarre antics of this remarkable little man.

The midget was now twirling a miniature silver gun, which he had produced from a neatly concealed shoulder holster. On cue, the tall man lifted the second bag and his small friend onto the cart. I didn't dare speak to my sister as our entire group was steered over to the customs inspector who watched, highly amused. Those in line ahead of us fell away as the acrobatic little fellow continued his athletic flips and spins atop our suitcases. "Make way, make way," he sang out, sounding very similar to Tattoo's "Dee plane, dee plane." At that moment, I did feel very much as if we had fallen into our own episode of *Fantasy Island*.

The gun twirling reached phenomenal speed — seemingly a display for the man behind the counter. When the little weapon finally found its way back to its holster, the officer slapped his thigh. "Wang Wang, you are as good as ever with that little thing," he said. Then, chuckling and shaking his head, he greeted Wang Wang's tall companion, Pete, and waved us through. Neither Carolyn nor I — nor our suitcases — were of the slightest interest to anyone.

Once on the other side of the customs barrier, Emilia rushed into action. She herded her new charges outside onto the curb and waved her lace handkerchief peevishly. "Bert! Bert! Bert!" she shouted in a voice accustomed to having its way.

In a wink, a black Mercedes pulled up and its driver hopped out. He and Pete loaded the trunk while Wang Wang, suddenly quiet and seemingly bored, stood beside the car, hands jammed into his tiny pockets, kicking at pebbles in the dust.

"Get in, get in! You must be tired, no?" our hostess chirped.

Carolyn, biting her lip, cast a long and dangerous what-the-hell-is-going-on look in my direction. I tried my best to ignore her. If this unfortunate soul was Emilia's son or relative, or even a friend, it would be appalling for us to lose control now, and yet that knowledge paradoxically made the urge to laugh almost unbearable. I crawled into the backseat beside Carolyn and sat by the window. Very briefly we were alone.

"Jeeze, Kath . . . "

"Shut up, shut up! I thought it was the baby!"

"I know, but who . . . "

The car door opened and I shoved my fist against my mouth and peered out the window. I wondered where the two men were going to sit as the girls and their mother piled in, filling up the air-conditioned vehicle. Bert took his place behind the wheel and Emilia lowered the window opposite mine just long enough to slip some money into the small, outstretched hand of Wang Wang. As we pulled away, that hand slid the money into a pocket while the other performed a smart military salute. I turned to look out the back window. Wang Wang grew steadily smaller as we rolled away.

On the road, Emilia proved to be a good tour guide. She worked hard to interest us in the statues of rebels and local heroes and the wide, treed boulevards we sped past as Bert set a course for one of the city's suburbs. I continued to look out my window, hoping my attempts to gain control would seem like avid interest in everything being pointed out.

Eventually I stopped hearing Emilia, wondering instead about Wang Wang. He and Pete were not part of Emilia's family, nor were they her friends. What they were was still uncertain, but the last glimpse I'd had of them was disturbing. I suddenly felt the way I did the year I outgrew the circus and realized that beneath the gloss and sequins and fancy lights were tired, ragtag people whose job it was to make strangers laugh for all the wrong reasons. Pete and Wang Wang, two men of very different height, had performed a service of some sort and had been paid for it. They had melted into the rich blackness of the night and only one word described my last glimpse of them — sad.

All need to laugh had completely vanished by the time we reached Emilia's family compound. We approached a high cement wall and drove slowly along its length for almost two city blocks. The glint of glass shards and barbed wire winked at us from the top of the wall as the headlights illuminated our way. Across the street, tumbledown shacks made of cardboard and tin formed a grey jagged line against the twinkling night sky. I hoped the forms scattered here and there on the sidewalk and on the curbs were sleeping people. If they weren't, they were corpses.

Then the car slowed even more and made a sharp left. Immediately, a high electric gate slid sideways, opening wide enough for our car to pass through. A heavily armed security guard stepped out of the doorway of his small shelter and saluted smartly as we passed. *Welcome to Manila,* my inner voice said, as my eyes began searching for a little girl whose name was still Mari.

13

"HELLO DARLING," I WHISPERED . . .

Once inside the compound walls, we drove past one huge, gracious house with white gingerbread verandas all around. Ahead of us, beyond a parking circle was another house, brightly lit, with a line of people waiting at the steps. I counted six cars, all Mercedes Benzes, making ours the seventh as we parked. To our left, across a wide rolling lawn, was a third house. Palm trees, flowering shrubs, and gardens, their colours taken by the night, waved gently in the breeze.

Like queens, Carolyn and I emerged from the backseat while Bert held the door open. Emilia immediately began introductions, starting with her "esposo," Buti. He smiled warmly and welcomed us to his home, hoping we would be comfortable during our stay. Buti was soft-spoken and very charming. Next came the three daughters who had not come to the airport, then Emilia's sister Elana, a couple of her children, and on down the line to Mama, who sat, regal in a rattan peacock chair, smiling sweetly.

"You must bless her like this," Emilia's youngest daughter

instructed me, as she stepped up to her grandmother, took the woman's wrinkled hand, and placed it on her own forehead. Following the example, Carolyn and I did likewise. This proved to be the right thing to do. Immediately the ice was broken and happy chatter rose up all around us.

The second line had yet to be introduced. Here we met Ethel the midwife, Baby the main floor helper, Millie the cook, Teeny the laundress, Nina the hairdresser, Banoy the yard man, Loretta the child psychologist, Piña the ya-ya (nursemaid), and Chico the dog. This impressive array, excluding Chico, was the staff of Emilia's immediate household and in my fatigued state, their names slid past, to be learned in stages over the next two weeks.

As everyone started filing into the house, Buti turned to his wife and said, "You see, I told you! We should have ordered special beds to be made. Look how big they are!"

Emilia immediately called for Baby and told her to order longer beds in the morning.

"Oh, no! Really that won't be necessary," I protested.

"Nonsense," Buti insisted. "If you can just put up with some discomfort tonight, we will have the situation remedied tomorrow."

"But we sleep in regular-sized beds at home . . ." It was no use. With a wave of his hand, Buti indicated it wasn't worth further thought and motioned us inside. I searched for Carolyn's reaction, but she studiously kept her eyes lowered.

We entered through sliding glass doors into a spacious, beautifully appointed, sunken living room. On the way into the family room we passed a low glass coffee table on which incredible lead crystal sculptures and gorgeous Lalique bowls were displayed. I estimated my entire apartment contents could have been purchased with the money invested in this collection alone.

Off to the side was a family room, where most of the meals and day-to-day family affairs were carried out. Emilia's five daughters sat close. They were all beautiful girls who seemed very eager to know us. The youngest appeared to be about nine and the eldest we would learn was nineteen. Already they were addressing us as Tita Kathie and Tita Carolyn. We had become immediate aunties.

Still, there was no sign of Mari.

Once into the bags, I produced the gifts that I had taken so much care to choose. In this setting they looked like suitable material for a garage sale. There were polite thank you's all around, but the only things that sparked any genuine interest were the boxes of maple sugar candy I had brought for the girls. These were sucked upon noisily even as Millie produced a huge plate of lumpia, small crêpes filled with lettuce and vegetables. Many glasses of Coca-Cola accompanied this treat.

"Eat, eat," Emilia urged. "You must be hungry after your travels, no? This is a very popular local dish. It can be your merienda for now. But if you are still hungry, Millie will prepare something for dinner."

I wasn't in the least hungry. In fact, I was beginning to feel light-headed and slightly nauseated. I only wanted to see Mari and go to bed. Dutifully I chewed the lumpia and washed it down with Coke. Finally, after more excruciatingly polite conversation, I asked if I could see the baby.

"The baby? You want to see her tonight?"

"Well, I thought . . ."

"Piña, Piña, Piña!" Emilia shouted. "Bring the child! Kathie will see her now!"

There was silence for a moment and then it was broken by wails of protest. "The child" had been wakened and she wasn't happy about it. Long moments passed and then I spied a yellow form, small for a toddler of twenty-one months, flit behind the kitchen door that opened into the family room. A giggle, a whine, laughter from Emilia's girls, a squawk all heralded Mari's unceremonious shove into the room. With legs braced, she tried to stand her ground, but was no match for the force of Piña's push.

For an instant Mari stood aghast, taking in what must have been the most terrifying sight of her young life. From what she could see, it was apparent that huge, white foreign devils had invaded the house and she was being offered up as their first sacrifice. Peals of unfeeling laughter greeted her fear.

Piña pushed and shoved Mari in my direction, increasing her distress. Baby, the main floor helper, rushed to me, spilling wrapped hard candies from her fist as she urged me to offer Mari one. Dumbfounded, I watched the performance.

"Please don't force her," I said, but my words were drowned in Mari's screams. Everyone seemed to think the whole scene was very funny.

The little girl was dressed much too warmly in yellow Dr. Denton sleepers, complete with feet and trap door. They were very much too large and the plastic soled feet of the garment were now dragging behind Mari as she continued to resist approaching me. The child was drenched in sweat and her face was shiny with tears and nose drippings. I couldn't really make out her features in the distorted countenance before me, but I could see that her hair had been recently shaved off close to her head, leaving a dark shadow of fuzz.

"This is your mommy. Go to mommy. Bless! Bless mommy. Mari, bless your . . ."

It was as if this dreadful scene was designed to retard our relationship badly. I stood, spilling the hard candies onto the floor and terrifying the poor little girl even more. "Please, let her go back to bed," I said as firmly as I dared. "We can get to know each other better tomorrow. I'm sorry I asked you to wake her. It was very stupid of me."

The sobbing child was immediately picked up and removed. Her cries were disturbing only to Carolyn and me. "She's a very beautiful child," I said to Emilia, for want of anything better to say.

Emilia threw her head back and laughed long and hard. When she recovered, she dabbed the moisture from her face with a lace hanky and said, "You surely must be looking at her through a mother's eyes, Kathie. But don't worry. I will show you the exercises for her nose. You must rub it each day like this. It will become respectable in no time." Mama nodded her wise agreement while I wondered what it was they considered so wrong with the tiny button of a nose that a Kleenex couldn't fix.

Thankfully the distant crying finally stopped. Even better, we were offered our choice of more food or bed. Both of us opted very quickly for bed.

"I hope you don't mind sleeping in the basement. We thought you should sleep in Mari's room. That way she will get used to you. Osmosis, you know? It will happen in the night."

At this point I would have happily slept in a graveyard, but I had to admit Emilia's idea was a good one and I was eager to undo the harm that had just been done. Perhaps, if we could be alone in a quiet room, the baby would get used to us from the safety of her bed. Perhaps, if we were lucky, she was already sleeping and we would look far less frightening to her in the morning.

The "basement," as it turned out, was only two or three steps down and was just as beautiful as the upper level. Our suitcases had already been carried into the bedroom at the far end and as we entered the darkened room, Carolyn and I assumed we were alone for the first time since our arrival.

Emilia switched on a small nightlight only to shatter that illusion. There were two beds in the room: one was empty and it was pointed out as Carolyn's; the other held Mari, asleep with a bottle in her mouth, propped on pillows and surrounded by the sleeping nanny, Piña. Emilia motioned for me to wait as she pulled a low trundle bed out from underneath Mari's.

"You will sleep here," she informed me. "Remember —

osmosis!" With that, Carolyn and I were left alone with Mari and Piña. We found our nightgowns and undressed hurriedly. In the dim lighting, I tried to examine the sleeping face of the little girl who was still very much a stranger, but it was half hidden by the bottle and further obscured by blankets. Exhausted, I lay down on the low mattress beside her and was almost asleep when a quiet tap was heard at the door. Carolyn answered it to find Millie smiling behind a huge tray of cold noodles and shrimp and more soft drinks. "You must have this in case you are hungry in the night," she said. My lips felt paralysed and rubbery as I tried to respond. Before the door was fully shut, I was asleep.

Some time later, the feeling of being watched was overpowering and I opened my eyes to see who was up. For a moment I couldn't make anything out in the dim light, but then I realized that my field of vision had been severely reduced by Mari's face floating about six inches above my head. She was glaring down from the edge of her bed, studying me as I lay sleeping on my back. The moment I understood what was happening, I smiled without moving. The serious face never moved or changed expression.

"Hello, darling," I whispered in what I hoped were low, soothing tones. This was the moment I had waited for. Our first contact.

Then, without the least warning, the child punched me squarely on the nose, illustrating graphically why they say you must hit a shark on the snout if it's in a feisty frame of mind. My body jerked several times as shock waves travelled up and down my spine, and as all the air left my lungs, I let out an unearthly noise. Mari retreated to the arms of her startled ya-ya. Carolyn groped for the light switch and ran for toilet paper from the adjacent bathroom as blood began to gush from my nose.

Mari was hysterical as Piña, uncertain of what had happened, held her tight and hugged the wall on the far side of their bed. Bug-eyed, she shouted volumes of something at the baby and at me, but it was in her native Tagalog and I understood only that she looked like she had seen a ghost.

"Kath! What the hell happened?" Carolyn shouted above the noise.

I mumbled my side of the story past the wad of toilet paper as the other two continued clutching at each other and shrinking away from us. The lights in the rest of the house came on and before long Emilia and her eldest daughter appeared in the doorway.

Emilia, all concern, shouted at the girl to call for a doctor, but I shook my head and insisted it wasn't necessary. Millie was roused and an ice pack was brought. I tried to make as little of the incident as possible, while gingerly testing my neck to see if it was truly dislocated or simply in a muscle spasm. I rose dizzily from my bloody cot and wafted past the crowd into the bathroom. This activity brought renewed energy to Mari's crying.

Cold water did much to stem the dizziness and I managed to staunch the bleeding before coming back out. By now, two more daughters were awake and Buti had stationed himself on the steps to observe and dictate instructions to his household. Piña was still quivering, certain, I supposed, that I had tried to kill her and the defenceless baby in their sleep.

Carolyn managed to explain the situation and vindicate me. We sat in the family room where Carolyn accepted a cup of tea. I had two painkillers. Once Baby had changed the sheets and the wailing from the basement had stopped, we decided it would be safe to return. Once again, I assured Emilia I was not in need of medical attention and we all went our separate ways.

In the bedroom-from-hell, the baby was quiet, but she was on the alert and definitely not close to sleep. Piña lay warily with her while Mari sucked on a fresh bottle of water and corn syrup. Aside from the two split seconds in the backseat of the car, my sister and I hadn't been alone for a minute. I was dying to get her perspective on what it was we had landed in.

The baby whimpered dangerously as we entered. Unwilling to approach my bed, I sat on Carolyn's at the far side of the room. We left the light on for everyone's security and spent the next hour or so sizing each other up in silence. The only noise to break the stillness was the clink of Carolyn's fork on the plate as she tucked into a healthy serving of cold noodles and shrimp. I looked at her in disbelief.

"I can't help it," she said. "Must be jet lag. I'm suddenly very hungry."

The lumpia we had eaten earlier still sat heavily in my stomach. "I may never eat again," I whispered, still observing Mari observing me.

"Kath, don't worry about the baby. She likes you, you'll see. Look how interested she is. She's going to be great when she comes around. She's got so much spirit — a real little presence. And look at those eyes! I like her a lot, already."

"Good for you," I said. "If you like her so much, perhaps you'd like to sleep in the deathbed over there. Go on. Maybe if you're lucky, osmosis will happen."

I had called her bluff. My sister declined the offer and we spent what was left of the night on her bed, dozing against the wall with all the lights on.

14

"TRY SOME BALUT, TITA KATHIE"

"Good morning! Good morning!"

I was awake, but I had no concept of what time it was, what day it was. There was a small window in our room covered by heavy drapes, which shut out any sign of day. It might be noon for all I knew. One thing was certain. However long we had slept wasn't nearly long enough. My head ached and my neck hurt as I sat up and looked around.

"Good morning! Good morning!"

Why is everything repeated twice here? I wondered, as Carolyn rolled to an upright position. The light was still on, but Piña and Mari had already left their bed. A glance at my wristwatch showed it was 7:30. Surely we couldn't have slept through to evening.

"Good morning! Good morning!"

"Whoever that is sounds like a bloody parrot," I groaned.

"It is a parrot. Look." Carolyn, standing on Mari's bed, held back the curtain just enough to get a glimpse of what was going on at the back of the house. Teeny, the laundress, was already up and in a flurry of activity, probably trying to remove all traces of violence from my bedding before the heat of the day became oppressive. Just in front of the window, an African Grey Parrot was standing on its perch, greeting the morning in a raspy voice. Relieved that we hadn't shamed ourselves by sleeping through our first day, we washed and dressed in quick order.

Breakfast was already in full swing as we entered the family room, trying to pretend we had slept well regardless of our rough start to the night. I glanced around, hoping to see Mari at the table, but no such luck. This was the day we would become friends, I was sure. In the clear light of day I was certain it couldn't be so dreadfully difficult.

"How is your nose, Tita Kathie?" asked Hope, the youngest of the girls.

"Oh, never better," I lied. In truth, I was having trouble breathing past the dried blood that still caked my nostrils.

The moment we sat, platters of food were passed down the table. If breakfast was meagre outside the walls of the compound, there was no shortage here. Mounds of sausages, plates of pork, fish, and beef, bowls of rice, and small packets wrapped in green leaves were all offered to us. To be polite, we took a small sample of everything, as Emilia explained its origins.

"This is the pork and the sausage from the pigs of my esposo. This is the fish of my sister's fish farm. This is the beef of my brother's cattle."

Then Felicity, the twelve-year-old daughter, passed a bowl containing strange-coloured eggs.

"Try some balut, Tita Kathie," she implored. "It is very good."

"All right," I said, taking one of the eggs. Carolyn got hers, leaving Felicity free to help herself. Eagerly, she selected her egg, whacked it open with a spoon, and sucked noisily on the end. Then she tipped it out and plopped something oily and solid onto her plate. Blackish liquid puddled around the lump that lay there.

"What kind of eggs are these?" I asked, trying to deny what I thought I was seeing.

"They are fertilized eggs. Felicity is eating the embryo, already," Emilia explained brightly.

And indeed she was, with great enthusiasm. I looked away as the unfortunate unborn hatchling skittered around the plate each time Felicity's knife threatened to slice into it. This was where I drew the line. Polite or impolite, I was not eating balut. I returned my unopened egg to the bowl and apologized. Carolyn did likewise.

Though we were offered many delicious and unusual dishes in the Philippines, and gamely tried them all, we never managed the balut, which continued to appear at breakfast and special lunches held in our honour. This, however, was the beginning of a wonderful relationship with Felicity. She quickly learned to station herself between Carolyn and me on every balut-likely occasion. That way we could accept it graciously, then slip it onto her plate once the conversation was underway. It was a mutually beneficial arrangement; we ended up being good sports and she ended up with three times her share of the delicacy she so relished. All I had to do was look diligently the other way and pretend I didn't hear the loud slurping beside me.

Later that morning, I spotted Mari through the partially opened door to the kitchen. She followed Millie around like a young puppy, hand held high in a begging gesture. Now and then a little mew of protest could be heard as the child continued to be ignored. Finally, Millie grew tired of having the child underfoot. She spread some condensed milk on a piece of bread and handed it to the baby, who scurried off and sat in the corner on the floor. Through persistent begging, Mari had just earned her breakfast.

"Why doesn't Mari eat with you?" I asked, as evenly as I could.

The question seemed to surprise everyone at the table. Emilia finally explained.

"She never eats with us, you see Kathie. She thinks I am the witch and screams when I come near." Emilia laughed. "She likes me almost as much as she likes you. You see? It is easier if she just stays away and plays with her ya-ya."

"But . . ."

Carolyn nudged me with her foot. I looked sideways and got her stop-now-before-you-go-too-far look.

"We are happy you are up," Buti said, changing the subject. We thought you would like to sleep a little longer, but now you can go to church with Emilia and the girls — if you would like to, of course."

I would have loved to sleep longer and was already wishing I had. Nevertheless, we said we would be delighted to go to church. Before we knew it, we were stepping into the family minibus. Emilia and her five daughters were already inside and Bert was at the wheel. Apparently Buti wasn't a regular participant in Sunday morning worship.

To my surprise, Mari, in a pretty but very large dress, sat upon Felicity's knee. She looked none too happy to see us, but aside from a single unpleasant squawk of protest, kept her composure and her silence. I smiled at her, hoping this was when we could start to make peace. She returned my offering with a stony stare and began to fiddle with the ribbon on her dress. She seemed to have struck a silent deal. As long as I kept my distance, I would be tolerated.

Felicity reached into her pocket and pulled out two candies. Unwrapping a green one, she popped it into Mari's waiting mouth. The other she gave to me, with a wise little wink. I put the candy in my pocket, refusing to buy Mari's acceptance with an orange sweet. Mari's expression changed from stony to stormy.

Obviously this child had been trained to expect little payoffs for performing well or badly. If she was good, she got a candy. If she cried and threw herself down, she got two or three in return for her silence.

I watched Mari carefully. Carolyn was right. She was interesting and had compelling eyes. They were large and round and fringed with long, thick lashes, but mostly they were dark and deep and full of mystery. Mari was smaller than she had seemed in the night. Her exposed limbs, now that they were visible, were toothpick-thin, and today she wasn't wearing diapers, making her appear even smaller. Only her cheeks betrayed any potential for baby roundness, and I was suddenly eager to have her home and gaining weight the way Lienne was doing so very far away. Once Mari's hair was a little longer, and once her sullen expression was gone, she would be very pretty indeed.

Felicity tickled the back of the baby's neck, and for the first time I saw a hint of a smile. Mari held the candy in one cheek, making her look like a tiny chipmunk. As the tickling increased, she threw her head back and laughed a dry cackle as if she was unpractised at merry-making of any kind. Lime-coloured saliva rolled down her chin and it was then I saw the dreadful condition of her mouth. Where her upper front teeth should have been were grey pulpy stubs protruding only slightly from the gum line. What remained of the others wasn't much better. They were pitted, discoloured, chalky little things that would certainly not serve her until her sixth or seventh year.

"What happened to the baby's teeth?" I asked Emilia.

"Oh, don't worry about them, Kathie. They are only the milk teeth already. It is of no matter. I can see you are the worrier of the family. Your sister is the calm one, but you are very nervous, no?"

This observation seemed to amuse Emilia and her children, but it didn't distract me from the subject at hand. I made a mental note to call a dentist at the first opportunity — that is, if Mari came home with us.

In the plaza in front of the huge cathedral, a large crowd had gathered around vendors selling an array of peanuts and sweets and helium-filled balloons. Inside, small children ran up and down the length of the nave, their brightly coloured balloons bobbing after them.

We arranged ourselves on a long pew, automatically avoiding all dangerous seating arrangements. Mari sat with Felicity, comfortably distanced from Emilia and me. From her vantage point she observed Carolyn and me sideways from under her dark lashes. Whenever our eyes met, she shifted hers away, feigning disinterest. Eventually, she noticed Emilia cooling herself with an ivory fan. Showing considerable resourcefulness, she seized the service program and followed suit, looking very pleased with herself as puffs of air blew short wisps of hair up and down on her forehead.

Rebecca, who was fifteen and seated next to me, whispered, "Mari has never been to church before. She is here to give thanks for her new mother. We will see how she behaves."

Mari behaved amazingly well. It was apparent that she had never been taken out much at all, and that she was enjoying the experience immensely. Nothing escaped her notice; she was a watcher. Not only that, Mari seemed to play life by her own set of rules. Whatever her story was, it was sad, but no one was going to mess with her. There was a presence and a certain dignity to this child, which I had to admire.

The service was long and mostly beyond understanding. It was conducted in Tagalog, leaving Carolyn, Mari, and me about equal on the comprehension scale. The incense and communion were familiar enough in any language, but beyond that, the service was an endurance test. I was beginning to feel the numbing drowsiness of jet lag when the offering began and Carolyn jabbed me sharply in the ribs.

"How much are you putting on the plate?" she asked.

I didn't need to look in my purse to know I had nothing small-er than one-hundred-peso notes. I wasn't sure, but I thought they were worth about twenty dollars, and in our careful financial condition, this seemed like too much. I relayed the message to my sister who began, as discreetly as possible, to rummage through her bag.

"Here, what are these?" she whispered, showing the tips and corners of assorted unfamiliar currency.

"I don't know, but it's not much. Just stick it on the plate. We'll figure out the money at the bank tomorrow."

"I wish I had an envelope," Carolyn muttered as she screwed up the paltry pesos in her hand.

Emilia and her daughters all sat poised with their personalized, sealed envelopes at the ready. The plates we were expecting didn't materialize. Instead, very deep nets resembling butterfly catchers on long bamboo poles were being thrust along each row of pews. Ours hovered closer, held at the far end by a squat woman with a watchful eye.

"Kath, I can't put this in! It's probably only worth about ten cents!" Carolyn the Calm was starting to sound alarmed.

"Just stick it in quickly," I advised, unwilling to part with one of my larger bills. "Push it down to the bottom so nobody will see it."

Finally the net bobbed in front of Carolyn. As discreetly as one could with a fist full of nothing, she stuck her arm well down into the deep cone of the net, hoping to deposit our offering and bury it among the others. I thought she was doing pretty well and smiled piously at Emilia in an effort to deflect attention away from my sister. And then all hell broke loose.

With a force that would have impressed the Exorcist, my sister's entire body rocketed sideways on the well-polished pew, wiping out the two older daughters and sending them to the floor with a terrific whumpf. As the tangle of people struggled to right themselves, Carolyn was laid out full length on the wooden bench, her arm still caught in the net. The woman at the far end of the pole was pulling and jerking the contraption wildly, making my sister resemble a hooked fish as she desperately tried to extricate her arm. Finally, the net-carrier, triumphant in her bid to save her collection for God alone, pulled the cash to safety and moved swiftly on to the next row. Emilia and her remaining three girls, envelopes still poised, stared incredulously. Even Mari leaned forward to get a better view.

I tried to assist Carolyn back to an upright position and finally she rose, ruffled and flushed with embarrassment. In an effort to regain my composure, I faked concern. "Are you all right?" I asked.

"Christ Almighty!" my sister blasphemed close to my ear. "She must have thought I was trying to steal the money." Carolyn sat rubbing the welt in the crook of her elbow where the hoop had dug in, while the others in our party continued to peer in silent wonder.

Magdalene, Emilia's eldest daughter, and one of the fallen, was the first to regain her composure and come to our rescue.

"Oh, my goodness, Tita Carolyn," she said, straightening the pleats of her skirt. "You must be very tired to fall over like that. You will need a rest before the reunion begins."

Reunion? There was no time for questions. The congregation was back on its knees, while the priest gave thanks for every last peso in his nets. Luckily, everyone prayed with their eyes shut. Only Mari witnessed how close my sister and I were to another appalling loss of control. She definitely was not amused.

Bert drove us home as Emilia gave us the next part of the day's schedule. "You must go home and rest," Emilia informed us. "I hope you will not mind, but every Sunday we have our family reunion. It may be a little confusing. In fact, the last person who visited us during a reunion fainted from all the noise. After your siesta you will sit with Ma where it is a little quieter, no?"

We dutifully agreed and staggered down to our basement refuge for one blessed hour of solitude, only to be met by the wails of Mari who had no intention of accepting us back into her lair. Her ya-ya had already removed the borrowed dress and, at the first sign of protest, had hurried to prepare another bottle of corn syrup and water.

With a sickening thud, I realized the miracle of osmosis would not happen this Sunday nor any other as long as Mari could flee to the familiar safety of the unfortunate young Piña. Barely more than a child herself, Piña had been given the onerous task of keeping Mari clean and quiet, a feat she accomplished with the aid of a washcloth and an unlimited supply of sugar.

Disheartened, I stripped to my slip and lay on the bed next to Mari's, unmoved by the crying above me. Prudently, I remembered to turn my face away before drifting off to sleep.

Mari and Piña were still dozing when we awoke an hour later. Carolyn and I could already hear the bustle of reunion in the air as we tiptoed out of the room and into the bright light of high noon. Outside our bedroom door, I began to notice details about the house I had missed before. Over to the left in a small alcove stood a remarkable statue of the Virgin Mary. She appeared to be very old and carved from ivory. Her face was exquisite and framed with soft brown hair. A step closer revealed eyelashes and semi-precious stones. A freshly cut flower lay at her feet. This statue, I would later learn, was only one of several in Emilia's home. Most of them were from Spain and were priceless antiquities. Emilia made a habit of collecting them, especially if they possessed human hair and eyelashes as this one did.

Carolyn and I emerged from the house and crossed the wide expanse of lawn, almost unnoticed. Everywhere, passels of little girls ran giggling together in fives and sixes. The gatekeeper admitted a stream of cars and minivans. Smiling broadly, uniformed servants scurried to help each other unload huge coolers of food. Tables had been set up on the lawn under the shade of the trees. Finally, Emilia spotted us and hurried over to make sure all introductions were made.

We were taken over to Mama, who sat smiling sweetly while a long line of children and adults waited to bless her. After showing our respect, we were seated next to her where we spent a wonderful hour getting to know her and Emilia's sister. For the first time since our arrival, I felt totally relaxed in their company. Ma was a sweet, gracious woman who seemed truly interested in us and our mission. I felt an immediate kinship with her and thought of my own grandmother more than once that day. Elana too, was very unlike her sister. She was obviously the religious one, the philosopher, the dreamer. As quick as Emilia was in her speech, Elana was slow, deliberate, and reflective.

People continued to arrive in bunches. It was hard to believe that every last one was a relative, but they were, all except for the table of nuns at the far side of the yard. Apparently there had once been a daughter or aunt who had been in the order, and though she was now deceased, it was still a tradition for all of the ancient sisters to join the family on Sundays.

Mama finally stood and gave us a tour of the grounds, punctuated by "the orchid garden of Buti and the religious grotto of Elana." There was a playground, which was now busily occupied by throngs of little ones, though Mari, I noticed, was not part of the crowd. Ma proudly announced that she had sixty-three grandchildren and great-grandchildren in total. All but one, remarkably enough, were girls. Well, there were really two other boys, but they were "imports" — the adopted twins of Margette — and therefore didn't qualify as familial male births. There were three more pregnancies in progress. Maybe one of them would be a boy cousin for young Manuel who was, understandably, treated very much like a little emperor.

Luncheon bells rang in unison and Ma, clutching my elbow, directed us to seats beside hers. A vast array of food spread before us, and as the guests of honour Carolyn and I were served first. What we tried to refuse was spooned onto our plates by Ma. The dreaded balut arrived, but with Felicity smiling on my right, I was safe. Long prayers were said and finally everyone dug in eagerly. My stomach was still heavy from breakfast. Jet lag seemed to have stopped my digestive system in its tracks. All I had done since our arrival was eat and pray, and now it was time to do it all some more.

As we dined, Ma explained to us that today the helpers of Margette had prepared most of the food. Each week, a different household was responsible for the spread and it had become a bit of a competition between staffs to see who could do the best job for the reunion. As the dishes were cleared, we were direct-ed to the sweet table and told we must hurry along because it was time for the men to go and play golf, while the women were due to visit Pa.

"Where is Pa, anyway?" I asked Carolyn. "Divorce doesn't seem to run in the family, so why isn't he here?"

"I don't know, but don't ask. Maybe he's in hospital or a home or something. We'll find out soon enough."

As the men drove off for their game, Emilia approached us with sprays of orchids. "Here. You must give these to Pa when you see him. They are the orchids of Buti and they are Pa's favourite flowers."

Again, Bert was summoned and away we all drove to the near-est cemetery where everyone had quite a lengthy chat with Pa. Carolyn and I deposited our orchids. Mama wept quietly with Elana beside her while Emilia related all current events and family news of the week to her father. Naturally, Carolyn and I featured big in the update. Finally, her duty done, Emilia fell silent as everyone stepped up, touched the headstone, and bade Pa farewell until next time. I felt only slightly awkward as I took my turn and muttered, "Nice to have met you," which was the only appropriate thing I could think to say. At this point I had to pretend I was in the Philippines alone, and that Carolyn was a total stranger. One look at each other would result in disastrous hysterics. It worked, but the day was still young and I hoped we would manage to get through whatever was bound to happen next.

Emilia waited until we were all settled back in the van to make her next announcement. "Now we are going to Malolos, the home town of my esposo. If we hurry, we will get there just in time for church and the reunion of his aunties. Then we will watch the religious procession of Santo Niño. You are very lucky to see it, Kathie, and after coming so far, I am sure the Baby Jesus will give you his blessing to become Mari's mama. The judge will certainly have to agree after this."

I smiled wanly as I tried to remember for certain if, and at what stage, I had told Emilia that I was not Catholic. I knew I had, but now I wondered if she could have missed the point somehow. I was beginning to feel slightly uneasy that religion was going to become an issue, either before or during the hearing. As if she read my thoughts, Hope asked what church I attended at home.

"Well you know, as I told your Mama, we don't go to church quite as often as you do. In fact, when we do go, we go to a differ . . ."

Carolyn elbowed me sharply in the ribs and I stopped talking to glare at her, only to realize that at some unseen signal, everyone had pulled out rosaries, and Hail Mary's were being recited in unison all around us. When they were finished, I decided it was best not to resume my personal exposé.

The drive to Malolos, though not terribly distant, took a fair length of time on winding roads and through dense traffic. Just before sleep overtook us, we were deposited in the ancient town centre in front of a small, stone church. There was a carnival-like atmosphere to the place as huge crowds filed into the square. Emilia hustled us inside, where we sat through another high mass. This time, without hesitation, I deposited my hundred pesos in the net. "What the hell," I whispered to my sister. "Twenty bucks is worth an arm any day."

At the home of Buti's aunts, we were introduced to his side of the family, which, like Emilia's, was also strong in numbers. Their house was old, traditional in style, and made of solid wood, pegged together without a single nail. It was a thing of beauty, open at both ends to the breeze that wafted through. A large balcony at the front overhung the street below. Painted on one entire wall of the living room was the family tree. It was an immense, spreading thing, still very much alive as new miniature portraits of every family member were still being added in oils.

Buti's aunties were thrilled to have visitors from Canada and welcomed us warmly with another feast prepared in our honour. "This is wonderful," I said, trying to sound grateful for the food before us. "But you know, we really don't eat very much at home."

This announcement was greeted with loud guffaws. "Well, if you don't eat so much, how is it that you grow so big in Canada?" one old girl sputtered. She had a point, but at the same time I was wondering how everyone here remained so tiny. The whole thing was academic, anyway. The meal had been prepared for us and we were going to eat it, hungry or not. Luckily, there didn't seem to be anything else on the schedule and we were allowed to pick slowly at our plates and enjoy being the centre of attention. We talked until dusk trying to fight off the effects of too much food and rampant jet lag. Then, as guests of honour, we were escorted out onto the porch, seated in two heavy wooden chairs right at the railing so that we could have the best seats in the house for the procession of Santo Niño.

From our elevated position we could watch the solemn spectacle as it snaked its way through the narrow winding streets of town. It advanced at a funereal pace, accompanied by small bands and muffled drums. Candles twinkled around the ivory statues and in the hands of those who marched beside each flower-covered float. Armed soldiers, carrying automatic weapons in place of candles, marched alongside to ensure the safety of each family's treasured Santo Niño.

For the first two hours we were truly interested. But then Santo Niño of the Children passed, followed by Santo Niño of the Fishermen, Santo Niño of the Harvest, Santo Niño of the Poor, Santo Niño of the Old, Santo Niño of the Infirm, Santo Niño of the Shoes . . . and still the never-ending stream of lights wound its way through the streets towards us. And dusk had brought us more than the procession. Throngs of healthy country-grown mosquitoes hovered and whined in the air above us, on the trail of fresh Canadian blood. They found it in abundance while Carolyn and I smacked and swatted away to no avail. I recalled telling our doctor that we wouldn't be travelling outside the city.

"What's the incubation period for malaria?" I asked my sister.

"I haven't a clue, but I hope it's short and that we have a lethal dose. It's the only way they're going to let us lie down."

"Very funny," I replied, watching yet another head of human hair and set of human eyelashes pass below us. "Who do you suppose donated all of Santo Niño's wigs and lashes?"

"They were probably plucked from victims of the Spanish Inquisition. Kath, I'm going to pass out right here, if this doesn't end soon."

I leaned against my sister's shoulder and together we supported each other to keep from falling sideways off our chairs. We gave up on the mosquitoes and let them celebrate the festival of

Santo Niño to their hearts' content. Our eyes drooped and our heads nodded until finally — a miracle happened. The last Baby Jesus passed and Emilia tapped us on the shoulders.

"Come, come, Carolyn and Kathie. The procession is over and we must get you two sleepyheads home so you will be fresh for tomorrow when you must get down to the business of preparing for court. It is a good thing you had this day of rest first, no?"

I glanced at my wristwatch. It was 12:30. We had been in the Philippines just over twenty-four hours and in that time we had been entertained by a midget, met half the population of Manila, prayed a year's worth, gained considerable weight, and given more blood than even the Red Cross would have thought wise. It felt like we had been away for a year.

15

"THESE ARE NOT YOUR FINGERPRINTS!"

By mid-morning of our second day, two things had become painfully clear. Mari was not going to get to know me or Carolyn as long as she was in this house with others she could run to for candy. Her true fear of us was subsiding and now she had learned to cry for effect. The harder she cried, the more she was encouraged — and the worse the whole thing got.

Nor would we be given straight answers about Mari or where she had come from. I tried more than once that morning, but got different stories or "I don't know" every time. I had arrived determined to learn as much about Mari's background and health as possible. Lienne's experience at the hospital had taught me that. All I could glean from Emilia was that the paediatrician her daughters went to had been seeing Mari, and he had stated she was healthy and developing normally. Finally, in one of our rare moments of privacy, Carolyn agreed with me that trying to find out the baby's background was important. "But," she said, "you obviously aren't going to get the true story from Emilia now. We've already heard so many lies that even if she did tell the truth, how would we recognize it? It comes down to this. You either want the baby or you don't. If you do, you might as well stop asking questions and take what you see at face value. If you don't, say so right now."

"Oh, knock it off," I responded hotly. "I can't leave her now. She's the most miserable, lonely little kid I've ever seen. I can hardly wait to get her out of here and into some sort of frame-work that makes sense. And what about her teeth? If I see one more candy go down her throat I'm going to throw up. They're ruining her health. I haven't seen one morsel of real food in front of her yet."

"I know. But Kath, she's never known anything else. Just wait. In only twelve days we'll take her back. The minute the plane door shuts, we can start, but don't rock the boat here. You'll only make it harder."

Carolyn was right and I had to swallow my frustration and wait. By the time we dressed, had breakfast, and got into the car with Bert and Emilia, I had calmed down considerably. Now, we were about to meet "a friend" before Emilia went to work. Once comfortable in the back, Emilia reached into a bag and pulled out a large round tin with a flamboyant bow on its lid.

"These are biscuits, Kathie. They are for my friend, but since you are the visitor, you must give them to her for her merienda. Can you say merienda?"

"Yes," I said, taking the tin. "These are for your merienda."

Emilia was ever so pleased that I seemed to be a quick study. Had she forgotten we had already had umpteen meriendas of our own? As I held the biscuits on my lap I noticed something tucked into one of the bow loops — a hundred-peso note.

Bert pulled up to a large stone building and drove through the entrance way. As we reached the front door, I realized we were at a hospital or nursing home. Quickly, Emilia led us down a corridor to an open office. Behind a large desk sat a smiling nun. She rose as we entered and greeted Emilia warmly.

Then it was my turn. "How do you do?" I asked as we shook hands. "These are for your merienda. I hope you enjoy them."

Smiles broadened on the faces of Emilia and Mother Maria Francesca. I still had no idea why we were visiting this woman, but assumed she was a friend of Emilia's who, for some reason, hadn't been able to come to the Sunday reunion. But once the biscuits were on the table, all pleasantries ended and we got down to business. "Let me see," the nun said to me as she opened her top drawer. "Ah, yes. Here it is. If you will just sign this, there will be no need to hold you up any longer."

Papers were shoved in my direction, but only the last one with the signature blanks was visible. The others curled back, held by a large paper clip.

"Of course," I said. "But first will you tell me what it is I'm signing?"

Mother Maria Francesca laughed heartily and Emilia chided, "There you go again, Kathie, always worrying. You are surely the shrinking violet of the family, not like your sister, no? You will give yourself ulcers like my esposo, already. This is just a paper we must have for the judge on Wednesday. Only a formality and nothing to bother yourself about. Hurry, sign now, and we'll let Mother get back to her duties."

I was upset. I looked at Carolyn as my hand hovered over the paper. She nodded almost imperceptibly, but I got the message: *don't rock the boat*. I scratched my name onto the document. Mother Maria then signed her name, but I noticed the witness and date blanks were still empty. The visit was over. As we got up to leave, Emilia stashed the papers into her purse while Mother Maria Francesca, all smiles, wished us a safe journey home and happiness with "the child."

Patient Bert was waiting and jumped into the car the instant he saw us emerge from the building. His next instructions were to take Emilia to her office.

"I'm sorry, Carolyn and Kathie, but I must go to the factory now. This afternoon you have another appointment at the police station. It is only routine. Those who will attend court must be first registered with the police. Bert will take you and wait while you do your business, then he will bring you home, already. You will be all right and I will see you when I return this evening. Then you will tell Ma and me about your adventures."

She offered no more biscuit tins with money-bows, so I assumed this was a more straightforward appointment. Emilia waved us off from the curb, the papers still safely inside her purse, and Bert began the long tortuous journey through Manila traffic. At this, Bert was clearly an expert. No visible lanes existed on the pavement and a river of vehicles of every possible description vied for space. Wherever there was a six-inch gap, someone stuck a bumper into it.

In Emilia's absence, Bert became something of a talker. He explained to us that a traffic analyst had been hired from Europe to come and set up a system of lights and one-way streets in order to alleviate the congestion of the city, but that after three weeks, he had thrown up his hands in despair, packed his bags, and left. Bert remained unruffled as he guided the shiny black Mercedes through a steaming sea of bicycles, rattletraps, and gaily painted jeepneys. An hour later, he manoeuvred it, unscathed, into the police station yard. I thanked my lucky stars for the blessing of "air con," as Emilia called it, when we stepped out and realized how hot the day had become.

The police station was a crowded cement block building that might have been in the back of beyond for all we knew. Bert had taken us far from the city centre to a run-down street somewhere in the suburbs. We approached the man at the desk inside the door and were told to wait until we could be interviewed.

The wait was unsettling. Dozens of unsavoury characters milled about or were ushered back and forth by police officers whose guns were at the ready. Still stinging from Emilia's shrinking violet remark, I tried to look tough and at ease, as if these surroundings were familiar to us. At least what Carolyn and I lacked in street smarts, we made up for in size. We were a good foot taller than the crowd of mini-thugs around us. I assumed an air of blasé disinterest towards all of them until one poor fellow was marched in under armed guard, his hands and feet in shackles and chains. He was a wild, demented soul, who had the look of Charles Manson about him. His eyes, bulging with desperation, scanned the room incessantly. Incoherent noises and spittle escaped him each time his head darted in search of the next victim. Naturally, his eyes settled on me, causing him to stop in wonderment for a moment. I smiled with what I hoped any madman would interpret as a neutral expression of encouragement or hope or friendship, whatever was needed most, then hastily shifted my eyes away before he decided to go for my throat. It didn't work. With a terrific roar, he started towards us, but was quickly jerked back by his keepers and subdued effectively enough to be pushed into another room. One bare foot and a shaggy lock were the last I saw of him as he fought to keep eye contact with me. The door closed firmly, muffling the sounds and thuds that continued for some time.

Eventually, we were led into a small chamber where our interview would take place. It was dingy and windowless, with one bare lightbulb hanging from a cord. High on the ceiling a fan spun lazily, not managing to stir the thick hot air around us. "A perfect place for an interrogation," I muttered to Carolyn, as images from *The Deer Hunter* popped into my head.

"Don't worry, it's all just routine. At least you aren't going to be dragged off like that other guy."

"Carolyn," I asked, "do you think I'm a chronic worrier? I mean, every time I ask what I think is just a sensible question, I'm told I'm good potential for ulcers from the neck down. Is it true, or is it just a smoke screen for —"

Carolyn never had a chance to answer. The door opened and in stepped the interviewer. He was in uniform and asked us grimly for our names, plunking his forms down on the table. The interview was surprisingly brief. I was asked where I was staying, how long I had been in the country, and what the purpose of my court appearance was. I handed over my passport so the man could record its number and the date of my entry to the country. Then he rose and beckoned us to follow him to a more public room where I was given forms to complete.

The forms seemed straightforward enough. I had to supply all personal particulars — home address, employer, physical description, etc. Carolyn looked over my shoulder as I dutifully filled in blank after blank. Without warning, she began what I recognized as one of her full-blown laughing fits.

"What in the world is the matter with you?" I asked.

Gasping and wheezing, she managed to point a finger at one of the questions I had just answered — Physical Build? Slight.

"Slight!" she shrieked. "Slight! Oh, Kath, that's a good one. Have you looked around lately? We have to be the two biggest women in the world right now."

In front of this man I felt an explanation was necessary, even though I could see that I was fully two and one-half times the size of the hardened criminals around me. I could have held my own in a prison riot. The police officer glowered at us, confirmed in his suspicion that I must be trying to pull a fast one. Even my sister was on his side.

"Carolyn," I reasoned in icy tones. "I have put five foot nine in the height blank, which I readily admit is tall. But they asked for build. Build refers to bone structure. I do have small bones. It has nothing to do with how —"

"Enough!" the man behind the counter said, drawing black lines through my daintily printed "slight" and spelling out L-A-R-G-E in heavy block letters. Then, as the papers were shoved under my nose, I was told to proceed down the hall to have my fingerprints taken.

The corridor was filthy and narrow, hardly allowing room for people to pass each other. Ahead of my large sister and me was a long line of criminal smalls. At the end of the line where I was to take my place, the dangerously insane man waited in the company of his guard, who was holding a long, impressive automatic weapon of some sort. When she saw him, Carolyn managed to straighten up somewhat and keep the noise of her inhaled snorts to a minimum.

I took my place behind the man, who by this time had been subdued considerably. His wide-eyed look was gone and now two hostile slits studied me intensely. I kept what distance I could as we inched our way to the fingerprinting table ahead. With great difficulty he was "helped" to produce a set of prints. Human contact was not one of his major likes; every time he was touched, or a finger was inked, there was a wrestling match. Finally someone handed me a card and shoved me along to take my turn.

A heavy-set woman seized my right hand roughly and ground each fingertip into the black sticky ink. Then, just as roughly, she smacked each finger down in its proper box on the card, making sure to squish and roll so that all the surfaces and sides of my digits left their patterns. For a moment I thought she was going for embossing. The left hand was next, and by the time she had finished, I could almost sympathize with the performance of the prisoner who had preceded me. Nevertheless, the whole thing was over before I could figure out why we had to go through this just so my petition for adoption could be heard in a civil court.

The next woman in the production line seized both of my hands and began washing them in what smelled like lighter fluid. Then she wiped them dry with the same inky rag everyone else had used, leaving my hands a smelly, blackish grey.

"Thank you, that's much better," I said.

"Hurry along! Pick up your card at the end of the table," the woman ordered.

I shuffled past the madman who was being wrestled to the ground again and seized my card. When I reached the exit sign an officer asked for it and the documents I had filled in earlier. I surrendered them readily and was surprised when the man responded with anger.

"These are not your fingerprints!" he bellowed. "Where is your card?"

"Why, yes they are," I said, holding up my smeared hands. "Look."

"You have picked up the wrong card and see here, what you have done! You have smeared the prints now with your dirty hands."

With that, the man began yelling for the person whose card I had picked up by accident. It was the maniac. One of the wrestling guards called for reinforcements, and with four people to assist, the process of printing Charles Manson was begun all over again. I found my own card among the others on the table, picked it up by the edges, and, expecting gun shots to ring out at any second, walked hastily towards the door.

Carolyn jogged alongside me. "Kath, you picked up that guy's card! I can't believe you did that!"

"All right, all right. It was a mistake. I'm a bit rattled, OK? I've never been fingerprinted before. And stop laughing at me right now. I bet this wouldn't be half so funny if it was you they were getting ready to put away."

Once out into the sunshine and heat, we found ourselves in a small enclosed dirt courtyard. The surrounding walls had once been whitewashed, but now were a nondescript mass of dirt, smears, and flaking cement. There were deep chips and gouges in the wall, which in my state weren't difficult to imagine had been made by numerous firing squads.

Another expressionless woman approached and handed me a long narrow slate upon which she had chalked a number. "Stand against the wall and hold this under your neck, like so," she instructed. "Your photograph will be taken soon."

I glanced over to Carolyn, shooting a strong warning that she should not even think of laughing, but when I saw her, I had to soften a little. She was doing her earnest best not to look the least bit amused and when she turned and walked away for a leisurely stroll around the yard, I knew she was losing the battle.

I stationed myself in front of a relatively clean patch of wall. Since there was no photographer in sight, I let my arms relax and held the slate down at my side.

It took a minute to realize that the woman was yelling at me.

"Hold your number in front of your neck!" I raised my arms again and held the slate in place until the photographer could come.

I almost missed her when she showed up. She was quite elderly and shuffled slowly out to where I stood. When she judged she was just the right distance away, she turned and raised her camera. I couldn't believe what she was using. I hadn't seen a camera like it since I was a kid. It was a pinhole box camera and it was aimed somewhere in my general direction.

The photographer was having difficulty locating my upside-down and reversed head against the end of the camera. Slowly, she scanned right, left, up, down. A small crowd of waiters and watchers was gathering. To avoid further embarrassment and delay, I began to swoop and weave, following the box, in the hopes that she would catch a glimpse of me before falling backwards, as she now seemed in danger of doing. At long last, she zeroed in and raised a finger to signal that she had found me. I glanced past her shoulder to see Carolyn, leaning weakly on the wall opposite me, this time with a Kleenex shoved against her mouth and an arm across her stomach. Even for me, it was too much. I began to smile.

"Do not smile at the photographer!" I was instructed from the side.

"I'm sorry," I said, lowering my number and spoiling the picture. "I'll try not to. Please ask her to hurry."

The tiny woman, her knees bent and body tense, prepared one more time to take my mug shot. Finally, I heard the insignificant click that was to make me a part of Manila's criminal records for the sake of posterity. I fully expected the next step to be a head shave and a dip in disinfectant, but to my astonishment, the slate was snatched from my hand and we were free to go.

As promised, Bert was waiting, and the two of us fell into the car. Carolyn was well past caring for my feelings now. "I wish I'd had a camera. Oh, Kath, I'm sorry, but that was the funniest thing I've ever seen."

"It's all right," I said. "I get the picture."

By the time Emilia's compound wall loomed large, we were almost back to normal. Ma was sitting in her special chair on the lawn, waiting to hear the news of the day. As I took her old, veined hand in one of my grey ones and pressed it to my forehead, I wondered what I could say to make sense of everything that had happened.

"I hope your day has been productive," she smiled as she greeted us like family. We sat beside the old woman and drank frosty glasses of iced tea. I took a long sip and to my surprise noticed Mari over by the house, walking hand in hand through the orchid garden with Buti.

Suddenly the craziness of the day seemed worthwhile. It was the first time I had seen Mari relate to anyone and it was good to know she could. The little girl I had come so far to see had finally shown herself. She looked contented. There, in that brief instant, she and Buti laid claim to one small ritual that was theirs alone. In a heartbeat, I knew Mari not only needed, but could make good use of, so much more.

Fingerprints and criminals were of no importance now. Without turning to the sweet, weathered face next to mine, I replied. "Yes, thank you. Our day has been very productive."

Mari stood on tiptoe and buried her nose in one of the delicate, ruffled blooms. Even as the conversation floated all around me, I began to plan how I would introduce her to more than the false promises of petals devoid of any fragrance.

This single, daily routine was all I ever saw Mari share with anyone. When it was over, she would be handed back to her waiting ya-ya, to be forgotten for another day.

16

"WHAT DO YOU THINK THE SENTENCE FOR PERJURY IS?"

Emilia had organized Carolyn and me first, which was her big mistake. We were told we had the morning to relax until it was time for Bert to drive us to meet with the lawyer. My plan almost formed by itself as I watched Emilia bustle about, instructing her staff before she left for the office.

Millie had been summoned to report what she had planned for the evening menu, pronounced "men-ooo" by Emilia. Baby had been told, in no uncertain terms, that the living room drapes were dusty and should be beaten. The hairdresser, Nina, was to be on deck for a dye job and a facial when Emilia returned at four; the manicure could wait until tomorrow. It was when she spoke to Ethel, the midwife, that the idea struck.

Ethel was instructed to take two of Emilia's girls to the paediatrician that morning. As they discussed what car and driver to take, I made up my mind to include Mari and myself on the expedition. That way I could speak to the doctor, tell him what was happening, and ask for Mari's medical records to take home with me. If I was lucky, the doctor might know more of Mari's origins than Emilia could remember. It was a stroke of genius, I thought. The shrinking violet had just found a way around the woman whose mind worked with the speed of light. I was very pleased with myself as Emilia waved goodbye and hurried out the door.

Carolyn eagerly joined in the plot and we waited patiently for signs that Ethel and the girls were ready to leave. As they headed for the door, I scooped Mari up and away from Piña and hurried to join them. The child was so shocked at this sudden physical contact that she took quite a long time before crying.

"It's all right," I told her. "Let's go for a nice ride in the car with Felicity and Hope. Then we'll come back home." I was surprised at how light she was.

Mari was much more used to Tagalog than English and I wasn't sure whether or not she understood me. Eventually she remembered to inhale a scream-sized breath and expel it close to my ear. I handed her to Felicity, and Mari stopped her protest abruptly, even without the enticement of a single candy.

Ethel looked startled as I told her we were coming too, but without Emilia there to thwart the action, she was not about to challenge us. Looking concerned, she led the way to the car park and told Bert to get the van, now that there were more of us.

Bert drove us to the brand new children's hospital, which was a thing of beauty. A large airy atrium was decorated on all sides with murals of children dancing together in colourful costumes. Hope told us as that this hospital was a special project of the First Lady. She had taken great pride in it and wanted it to be something she would be remembered by. The murals depicted the dances and children from different regions of the Philippines. Imelda Marcos was already resented by many who considered her expensive pet projects next to useless, but I had to admit this one looked pretty good. The cafeteria was made like a toy train. The reception desk and various pieces of furniture were giant pieces of fruit. This was a fun place to be sick, all right. The fact that it was almost empty of people barely entered my consciousness.

We took a seat on a large banana and waited until Felicity and Ethel were called in. Mari, perched on Hope's lap, even allowed me to smile at her and play "Creepy Mouse" twice up her arm before she remembered we were not friends and pulled away. We were making progress.

Finally, both girls were finished and the doctor opened the door to see them off. Carolyn and I walked over quickly and pushed past Ethel.

"Excuse me, Doctor," I said. "Could we speak to you for a moment? It won't take long." The door closed behind us and the doctor in the white lab coat waited for an explanation.

"You see, I'm adopting Mari and taking her to Canada. I thought you might tell me about her background and medical history. I'd like her records to take back, if that's possible, so her new doctor will have a record of her immunizations — that sort of thing." The doctor was looking doubtful, so I added, "If you can't get them ready right now, I'll give you the address to send them to."

The poor man was genuinely baffled. "Who are you?" he asked.

"I'm sorry," I said, backing up a little. I introduced myself and explained the situation more clearly. The doctor opened his door and peered over at Mari, then he closed it again. "I have never seen that child before in my life," he said.

"But I was told you had been treating her for some time."

"I'm sorry. Whoever told you that was confused. She has never been a patient of mine. She has no records here."

Carolyn and I had no choice but to leave empty-handed. Ethel looked like her throat was about to be slit as we all piled into the van and returned home.

Emilia had lied about the doctor and there wasn't much we could do about it. Carolyn and I had to return to our stance of the previous day. There was no sense asking answerless questions only to rock the boat. Court would be in the morning and then I would have the one important answer I had come for. Ethel didn't say a word to us about our aborted mission, and we never knew if our little indiscretion was reported to Emilia or not.

Fortified with tumblers of Coke and helpings of pork adobo, rice cakes, and leche flan, we were once again in the back of the car driven by Bert on our way to see the lawyer. I was beginning to feel comfortable with him. He was quiet and did his job without question, but by the back of his head, which is all I usually saw, I could tell he was a listener and a thinker. He only spoke when spoken to, but opened up considerably when given an opportunity.

We gave him one that day, and learned that the children's hospital had been in operation only a short time. It was, to all intents and purposes, empty, because hardly anyone could afford to go there. Hospitals, Bert pointed out, were very costly and that one in particular was extremely expensive.

"The First Lady has built this as her memorial and that is all it is good for. She even hired actors to play sick for the television cameras at the opening."

"Actors?" I asked.

"Well, not really actors. They were street children, washed clean and placed in beds so that the public would think the facility was useful. Afterwards, the children were given a few pesos and turned out on the streets again. The truth is, today the beds are empty. When the Holy Father tours next month, you can be certain the hospital will be full of patients again."

We were on a wide avenue full of traffic and people. Down one side a vast expanse of whitewashed plywood wall was being constructed. Bert pointed it out as another of the First Lady's ideas.

"This has been put up to hide the shanties behind it, when the Holy Father passes this way. Imelda Marcos does not want him to see the poverty in our country. The slum children will decorate it with paintings for His Holiness, so he will not see our shame."

"It seems to me it's exactly what he should see," Carolyn said. Bert agreed and then told us he was hoping the Pope would relax the church's stand on birth control. He had eleven children.

The conversation was just getting interesting when Bert indicated we were at the home of Attorney Corazón. He turned sharply and nosed the vehicle through an open gateway. "Come to the gate when you are finished and I will see you," he promised out the car window as he reversed carefully.

Carolyn and I were left standing in a scrubby dirt yard, bare of garden or decoration. One tall, spindly tree stood in the centre giving shade, if not beauty, to the house. Over by the front wall I noticed a cage on stilts. In it was a mangy dog who looked too hot and malnourished to snarl a warning that strangers were about. Underneath, something grey and cat-sized scurried around the corner. Only after I saw the bare tip of a tail whipping after it did I realize it was a rat.

We knocked on the locked screen door and waited a very long time until the shuffle of feet and a dry cough could be heard. Then from the poorly lit interior, we could make out an elderly woman coming towards us.

Attorney Corazón hardly gave us a glance as she opened the door, turned her back, and asked us to follow her into the sitting room. "You are a bit early," she informed us. "Sit down, be comfortable. I will see you presently."

Carolyn and I chose seats, though it was difficult to be comfortable in them. Every stick of Attorney Corazón's furniture — including satin throw cushions, crocheted ruffles and all — had been tightly wrapped in heavy, clear plastic. Until I began to sweat, making it quite sticky, the seat beneath me was so slippery that remaining upright was a challenge. Carolyn, clutching the arms of the chair opposite me, was already assessing the probability of being crushed to death by one of the many filing cabinets that tilted dangerously inward from every wall of the room. The plank wooden floor was straining to support all of Attorney Corazón's papers plus the added burden of two newly arrived giantesses. Maybe it would be better to slide onto the floor than to keep hunching back up onto my settee, which made the cabinet behind me rock dramatically. Piles of papers had been put on the coffee table in front of me, but it too had been protected from the elements by layers of sandwich wrap. The entire room had, for some reason, been mummified.

Attorney Corazón had gone to the far end of the room and seated herself in full view at a kitchen table. She didn't appear to be eating or busy with anything, but she kept us waiting until the appointed minute. Then she rose and on pink-slippered feet shuffled purposefully towards us, bouncing the floor boards ominously.

"So, now, which of you is it who wishes to become the mother?"

"I do," I said, fighting the urge to raise my hand.

Attorney Corazón sat next to me and we studied each other for some time. I don't know what she saw, but I, certainly, was looking at a most unusual face — one that seemed vaguely familiar. I couldn't quite put my finger on who she reminded me of. The dark wig she wore sat shiny and hat-like over large, heavy-lidded eyes — wise owl eyes that tilted down, giving the impression of great sadness. The nose between them was razor-sharp, long, and rather beak-like. Lips that had once been sensuous now sagged at the corners, apparently lacking the energy to summon up a smile more than once a month or so. She would have been a wonderful character actress, I thought, and then it dawned on me who she looked like — Peter Sellers, aged, in drag.

She shifted slightly and took a deep breath. "We must begin, Miss Cole. You must be at the court on time tomorrow morning and you have much preparation to do." Attorney Corazón produced a pair of bifocals and balanced them on her nose. "Let me see," she said in a deliberate voice, while she shuffled through a pile of papers on the table. "Yes, here we are. These are the questions I will ask you in court. They are marked with a Q. And these are the answers you will give. They are marked with an A. Do you understand the system?"

I think my yes was a given. Attorney Corazón was already instructing me on courtroom etiquette. "You will dress suitably, you will not chew gum, and you will answer always with 'Yes, Your Honour' or 'No, Your Honour.' I trust you have registered with the police, already?"

"I did that yesterday. It was quite an exp —"

"Good. Now read the answers and then we will rehearse everything together." Attorney Corazón handed me sixteen pages of script, crossed the floor, and put the kettle on to boil.

The first page started off all right:

Q: What is your name?

A: My name is Kathryn Cole, Your Honour.

Q: Where do you live?

A: I live in Toronto, Canada, Your Honour.

Q: What is your birth date, citizenship, marital status . . .

A: Your Honour . . . Your Honour . . . Your Honour . . .

Then things got interesting.

Q: Where are you staying in the Philippines?

The answer given under A was incorrect. It wasn't Emilia's address. I made a mental note to bring it to the lawyer's attention.

Q: How long have you been in the Philippines?

A: Six months, Your Honour.

I would have to tell Attorney Corazón that was wrong, too.

Q: Can you identify this document? (produce exhibit E)

A: (study exhibit E) Yes, Your Honour. It is my home study, completed in Canada.

Q: Can you identify this document? (produce exhibit F)

A: (study exhibit F) It is my home study completed in Manila, Your Honour.

Good Lord. A quick glance down the list revealed more discrepancies. Frowning, I glanced up at Carolyn. The plastic squeaked as it tried to grip my now-moist arms and legs. I pulled free and handed the list to her. Carolyn read enough to get the picture, raised her eyes to mine, and returned my frown.

"Excuse me. Attorney Corazón? There must be some mix-up here. This is not the correct information," I said.

The old woman sighed and came to sit beside me. "They are the correct papers. What is the problem?"

"Well, for one thing, I am staying at Emilia's home, not at this address."

"It is of no importance. You will give this address."

"But I don't know whose address it is. Besides, I have only been here three days, not six months."

"It is only a technicality. It would be better to say six months."

I was beginning to panic. "But what if they ask for proof? My passport was stamped three days ago! I showed it to the police yesterday. They wrote it down. What's wrong with the truth?"

"There is much wrong with the truth if it will not bring you the child," the lawyer countered. "You were ill-advised to reveal so much to the police. But what is done is done. We will just have to hope it does not complicate matters."

I could feel my throat tightening and felt chastised for not automatically assuming I should have withheld information from the authorities. Hell, it had been hard enough cooperating with them. I scanned down the list to the next point.

"I never had a home study done in Manila. What is exhibit F?"

Attorney Corazón shuffled through the large pile of documents in front of us. I saw some of the forms I had been sending Emilia over the last year. They gave some reassurance that I was at least the right client. "You most certainly have a home study. Everything is prepared. Yes, here it is."

In my hands I did indeed hold a home study. It described visits to my fictitious address over a period of six months. The signatures on the last page belonged to Mother Maria Francesca and me. But someone had been busy since I had seen them. The witness blanks were signed by people I hadn't seen and the paper was dated three months earlier. My stomach churned. Looking back at the question and answer sheets, I found more technicalities that needed addressing.

"Here. You are going to ask me to identify exhibit H, Mari's birth certificate. I've never seen it."

Patiently, Attorney Corazón rifled through the stack again. The document was a copy. The signature of the mother was a totally illegible backhand scrawl.

"All right," I said. "The next one is the adoption consent form. Could I see that?"

I was trying the lawyer's patience. "Miss Cole," she said as if she were indulging a little child, "you have a lot of memory work to do. I advise you to stop questioning the exhibits and get down to it."

Nevertheless, the form (exhibit I) was found and given to me. The signature of the mother on this paper was completely different. The first initial was large and elegant. It was followed by letters just as illegible as the others, but this time, they all followed the same slant to the right. Two signatures from obviously different hands were supposed to be written by the same woman. I glanced at the practice sheets.

Q: Whose signature is on the paper?

A: The mother's, Your Honour.

Q: How do you know it is the mother's?

A: Because I saw her sign it, Your Honour.

I put the paper down. "Attorney Corazón, these signatures don't match. Any judge can see that. You are asking me to stand up in court, take an oath, and say I saw the mother sign this document. It's not only a bald-faced lie, it's a stupid lie, and one I'm not going to get caught in."

Attorney Corazón adjusted her specs, tilted her head back slightly, and uttered an exclamation of surprise. "You may be correct. Yes, yes, it is a point. Well, no worry. We don't need the birth certificate." The old hands immediately began to tear up the exhibit. "Tonight you must buy a little white dress, find a priest, and have a nice Christening. We will use the baptismal certificate instead."

"But I'm not . . ."

Attorney Corazón removed her glasses and looked at me with a very tired expression. "Miss Cole, I have arrived at the age of seventy-eight years. I am old and I must make good use of the time I have left. You have everything you need except the priest. My advice is this: decide if you want the child. If you do, go home, have your Christening, and bring the paper with you to court tomorrow. When you arrive, be certain your memory work is complete and that you are concerned about more important things than little white lies."

With that, she stood up, nodded to each of us, and walked into her kitchen. Clearly our audience was at an end. Carolyn and I peeled ourselves carefully from the chairs and exited by the front door. My sister remembered to scoop up my homework.

Out in the yard, I exploded. "I'm not doing this! What the hell is going on here anyway? Carolyn, I'm not going to jail because that old bird wants me to say outrageous things that never happened."

"I know, I know," Carolyn soothed. "Calm down. We need to

go somewhere and order a drink. I've never wanted a lousy beer so much in my whole life."

We walked to the gate and Bert appeared like our magic genie. He knew just the place and took us there immediately. I was so wound up, I could hardly choke down the first sip.

"Why does everybody keep asking me if I want the child? Damit! I've come halfway around the world to get her and every time I ask for explanations I'm entitled to, they act like I can't make up my mind. What do you think the sentence for perjury is in this country?"

"I don't know. We need to go home and talk to Emilia. We'll tell her you're concerned and don't want to lie in court. If that means a new lawyer, I'm sure she can come up with several. Maybe we should call Malaya's father and go and see him."

"Forget it. It's too late. Besides, we have a Christening to attend." I was on the verge of tears.

Carolyn smiled. "The way things work around here, we may already have missed it."

I had begun to sniffle loudly so Carolyn ordered two more beers. They were the best beers in the world. My sister knew me well. She let me ramble about Mari, about Lienne, about prison, about fingerprints, about the Pope. I could be dangerous in this kind of mood and it was best that I got it out of my system before we faced Emilia. Finally, it was as good a time as any to leave.

We stomped through the living room, ready to do battle. Emilia emerged, fresh from her facial and "hair-do." One look at us, sparked the first real concern I had seen on her face yet.

"What is it? What has happened, Kathie?" she asked.

"Emilia, we have met with the lawyer. She wants me to say all sorts of falsehoods in court. Nobody will tell me what is true or why I should lie. I want Mari, I do. But she isn't attached to me yet. It might be better if I stop this right now and just pack my bags and go."

Emilia sized up the situation quickly. This was no time to tell me I was just a worrier. She switched tracks. "Of course you don't have to lie. Why do you think you should lie?"

"Because this is what Attorney Corazón wants me to say tomorrow." I handed the papers to Emilia. She read them and smiled broadly.

"You don't have to say anything you don't want to, Kathie. Nobody will force you. I will phone Attorney Corazón right now and tell her no lies. Only the truth will do. All right? You do not need to pack. You need a cool shower and a little merienda. And then you should retire early so you can be ready to become a mother tomorrow, no?"

I waited until Emilia dialled the attorney's number. Listening was next to useless, because the conversation was in Tagalog. The odd word of English crept in and I heard my name now and then. Eventually, Emilia hung up.

"It is all right, Kathie. Attorney Corazón understands. No lies. I will come with you tomorrow to the court. Now have your shower and get a good rest. I expect this is all because you are only overtired, yes?"

I hadn't expected her to cave in. Meekly, Carolyn and I sought the refuge of our room. Mari was there with Piña. I watched her sucking hungrily on her corn syrup and water. I wondered if I was out of my mind to be here at all. Food was delivered to the door and I ate mine, glancing at the script one more time. Finally I was calm, now that I understood memorizing it was unnecessary. I fell asleep, the rolled-up papers at my side.

17

"SHE IS GOING TO FAINT. SHE IS WHITER THAN HER SUIT."

Mari slept fitfully all night, which meant Carolyn, Piña, and I did, too. Each time she mewled Piña was up to prepare another bottle. In the morning there were four empties on the dresser and one in the bed. I wondered if Mari sensed that her destiny was hanging in the balance.

I probably wouldn't have slept well, anyway. After the first hour or so, I was wakeful even when the baby wasn't. I lay there wondering what Lienne was doing so far away. With a twelve-hour time difference, she no doubt was also awake.

I was relieved when morning finally came and we could get up and ready for the hearing; at least it was something to do. I found my stockings, long-sleeved blouse, and suit and got into them. The shoes, comfortable enough in Canada, pinched now that my feet had expanded to summer size. It was already very hot, though the sun hadn't been up long.

Before leaving the bedroom, I found the stuffed penguin I had brought for Mari. This was the first time I thought I could give it to her without a scene. Quietly I approached the bed where she sat solemnly. She watched as I sang and made it dance, but wouldn't take it. Feeling foolish, I put it down on the bed close to her. "He's yours, Mari, for good luck." Mari wanted that toy. But still very much her own little person, she would not accept it as long as I was in the room. After holding her for such a short time the day before, I was dying to pick her up again. But I didn't quite have the right yet. I hadn't even allowed myself to call her Miguela, though others in the house were using it inter-changeably with Mari. Such liberties would be tempting fate. I said goodbye and headed for the breakfast table.

Magdalene and Rebecca sat talking to Carolyn, and as I came in they all declared I looked very nice. Emilia was nowhere to be seen. I ate my breakfast, assuming she had overslept, but when it was time to go, she still hadn't turned up.

"Where is your mother?" I asked Rebecca as Bert pulled up at the front of the house.

"I'm sorry, Tita Kathie, I don't know. She left the house very early this morning. Perhaps she will meet you there. Bert is to take you to Attorney Corazón's house and pick her up along the way."

I felt strangely abandoned as we got into the car. This woman who had gone to no end of trouble to bring about the adoption was a total mystery to me. She had worked for a year getting things ready for this day. Here we were at her insistence, staying as guests in her house, eating at her table, and indebted to her forever. Then there was the appalling way Mari was handled and all the manipulation that came so naturally. Little waves of anxiety played within me as I wondered why Emilia had bailed out at the last moment. Did she have a premonition of disaster? Had she simply become bored with the whole affair?

The girls and some of the staff stood outside to wish us luck.

Piña, holding Mari, was at the front of the line. She lifted the baby's arm and waved it. With the other hand Mari clutched her penguin. As the car passed through the gates, I strained to keep her in sight. I was painfully aware that the next time I saw her, I would either be her mother or a soon-to-be-forgotten stranger who would have to walk out of her life forever. All the way to Attorney Corazón's house I visualized both outcomes, but was unable to decide which was the more likely.

◄o►

I could hardly believe the transformation in Attorney Corazón as she walked through her front door and towards our car. She was still old, but beyond that, she was quite changed. The shuffle was gone and she stepped quite smartly, sporting low-heeled leather pumps and a smart dress. She was even wearing her own salt and pepper hair, neatly wound into a French roll, and much nicer than her at-home wig. She carried an attaché case, which no doubt held her notes and a complete set of documents — minus the dubious exhibit I, that is. Attorney Corazón sized me up and seemed to approve; at least I had remembered not to chew gum.

"Good morning," she greeted us solemnly. "I trust you slept well." No mention was made of last night's call from Emilia and I assumed she was comfortable with our new understanding. The air conditioning was on full blast, keeping my body temperature and blood pressure somewhere near normal. "Where is your sponsor?" Attorney Corazón asked.

"Emilia?" I asked. "I have no idea. She was gone when I got up this morning." Attorney Corazón rolled her eyes skyward and muttered, "Mary, Mother of God, preserve us," which did little to settle my nerves.

The drive was much longer than I thought it would be. The courthouse was somewhere outside the city and was singularly unimpressive: a cement block building with a corrugated metal roof. The doors on opposite sides of the building were open, allowing whatever air might stir to pass through. A large photograph of Imelda Marcos hung on the front wall. She stood smiling regally in a butterfly sleeve gown, bejewelled, young, and about twenty pounds lighter. It was easy to see how Ferdinand had fallen for his beauty queen. Rough wooden benches were for spectators and Attorney Corazón indicated we should sit on one close to the front.

Though court had not yet started, the room was far from empty. A large group of Pilipinos milled about, apparently in a state of confusion. They had all been shouting and arguing when we entered, but they stopped, mouths agape, as Carolyn and I sat down. The most formally attired individual in the bunch wore a sweat-stained undershirt, nylon shorts, and old rubber thongs. Most of the men were bare-chested and so was one woman, who nursed a rather large child. I tried to outstare them in the hope that they would be embarrassed enough to look away and return to their squabbling. It didn't work.

Attorney Corazón leaned close and mumbled through clenched teeth, emphasizing the significance of what she was about to say by flashing the whites of her eyes. "Whatever you do, say nothing to anyone. And try to look inconspicuous."

It was a peculiar request under the circumstances. I would have to strip to the waist, shrink ten inches, and change more than my hair colour in order to obey. I nodded my compliance anyway, and looked down at my creamy silk suit, thanking whatever guardian angel was watching the day that I had decided against a hat.

Attorney Corazón read the docket and informed me that there was only one case besides mine. Thirty-seven squatters were to be evicted from a piece of land. The thirty-seven still eyed us with mistrust.

As we waited for the judge to appear, a few more people filed in. All of them wore the uniform of well-turned-out law clerks: navy double-breasted jackets, dress shirts, and grey pants. And all of them came and sat on the bench directly in front of us. Two nodded and one said a pleasant "good morning."

"Good morning," I answered automatically, not having the faintest idea who he was.

Attorney Corazón elbowed me sharply in the ribs and glared disapprovingly at me. "Sorry," I whispered, almost certain I hadn't revealed anything that would hurt our case.

"I wish you good luck with your petition," the young man offered.

Afraid to say thanks or even nod for fear of retribution, I let my eyes waft vapidly to Imelda's portrait. Attorney Corazón was looking wary and alert, as if something out of her control was happening, when yet another young lawyer entered the room and sat beside Carolyn.

"My Lord, my Lord," our counsel muttered. "Too many cooks. Too many cooks spoil the broth." This ominous platitude only confused me further. Carolyn, who had not been warned to keep silent, and whose ribs were protected by me, happily engaged the young man in conversation.

"Don't worry," she whispered in my ear. "They've been sent by Malaya's father to monitor the case. Isn't that nice!" I felt somewhat better to hear this, but obviously Attorney Corazón thought their presence drew too much attention and made us appear suspicious. Not that we weren't.

At long last, the judge was announced and we all stood.

The squatters fought as if their lives depended on staying put. I found myself silently rooting for them, but they were not represented by anyone and lost their case in record time. The judge was ruthless as he ordered them to abandon the property within twenty-four hours. The thirty-seven displaced people filed out and the judge looked around to see who was next. The room was empty of everyone except Carolyn and me and our sizeable legal contingent.

Suddenly Attorney Corazón was up on her feet reading the petition. Carolyn squeezed my hand as I received the signal to come to the front and step into the witness box. I looked around, but there was still no sign of Emilia. The Bible was placed under my left hand and somehow I found the voice to swear an oath to tell the truth. I did it in all good conscience.

Attorney Corazón almost smiled, giving me the impression that we were both on the same side.

"What is your name?"

"My name is Kathryn Cole, Your Honour."

"Where do you live?"

"I live in Toronto, Canada, Your Honour."

Attorney Corazón looked satisfied.

"What is your occupation?"

"I am an art director at a children's publishing company, Your Honour." I was getting the hang of things and just finding my rhythm, when suddenly the rules changed.

"Where are you staying in Manila?"

I gave Emilia's address, but before the last words could be uttered, the lawyer shouted the false address I was supposed to have memorized. There was an embarrassing pause and a deadly scowl from Attorney Corazón.

"How long have you been in the Philippines?" she asked in a less friendly tone.

"Four days, Your Honour," I stated, still believing I could tell the truth.

"Six months, Your Honour!" Attorney Corazón shouted, drowning my answer with her louder one. Her eyes narrowed and her head jutted forward. Apparently she was very displeased and shooting silent warnings to follow the script.

"Can you identify this document?" Exhibit A was handed over.

"Yes, it is my home study completed in Canada, Your Honour."

A smile. We were back on track. "Do you recognize this document?"

I held the bogus papers in my hand wondering what to do. "Well, I have seen it before, but —"

"It is my home study completed in Manila, Your Honour!" Attorney Corazón was either livid or panicking. I looked past her and down at Carolyn as a trickle of sweat ran down my back. Carolyn looked very worried.

"Can you tell the court what this is?"

"It is a signed adoption consent form, Your Honour."

"Who signed the consent form?"

"I was told —"

"The baby's mother, Your Honour!" Attorney Corazón was a one-woman team.

The court recorder's eyes rolled dramatically over the top of a mask-like affair she was speaking into.

"And how do you know it is the mother's signature?"

I pictured the roll of papers lying on the dresser where I had left them. Acting on the promise I did not have to lie, I had barely glanced through them once, making no effort to commit anything to memory. Even if I wanted to revert to the script, I would be in trouble sooner or later. I had to decide now how to continue. My lawyer had already lied for me and I was well into the fictitious scenario. "Because I . . . ummm . . ."

"I am sorry, I didn't hear you clearly. Did you say you saw the mother sign it?" Attorney Corazón asked.

The court recorder tore off her mask. "Your Honour," she implored. "Please instruct the witness to speak for herself. I do not know which answer to record."

I looked over to the judge. He appeared to be totally bored and disinterested in any answers at all. Leaning on an elbow, he rolled his head sideways and directed me to speak for myself.

"Yes, Your Honour, I'm trying." But before there was another question to deal with, Attorney Corazón spilled all the exhibits, A through M-1, onto the floor.

"Oh dear, how clumsy. Please excuse me, Your Honour." The old woman bent slowly down and took a very long time pushing and shoving the papers into a wrinkled mass. Periodically, her eyeballs left the job at hand and rolled meaningfully in my direction. The performance went on at some length. I was perspiring wildly and understood the lawyer was giving me time to re-group and make my decision. Her words from yesterday played in my head. *There is much wrong with the truth if it will not bring you the child . . . Decide if you want the child . . .*

Attorney Corazón walked over to a table and made a great show of trying to re-order her papers, all the while appearing to grow very senile. She mumbled and shook her head about her missing exhibit I. Pulling out her glasses, she walked over to the recorder and asked her if she could find it. She couldn't, of course; it had been shredded the previous afternoon.

"I'm sorry, Your Honour," Attorney Corazón sighed. "I have misplaced the child's birth certificate." She flashed an apologetic smile. "May I beg your indulgence to return to the matter later? I know it is here somewhere." With that, the sly old fox spilled half her papers again.

The judge shifted in his chair. "Certainly. Just get on with it or the child will be ready for university before we leave this room."

It was such a wonderful ploy, I decided to assume my role, whether I understood it or not. I stood, like a poorly prepared student ready to cheat if I had to, in order to pass the test. I hoped the answers I had glanced at so quickly would come back to me when I needed them. Feeling very close to spontaneous combustion, I struggled to breathe evenly.

"Miss Cole, how did you come to meet the infant's mother?"

I knew the response to this one. Just as I was about to open my mouth, there was a disturbance at the side of the room. Emilia had arrived in a noisy flurry of silk ruffles and a clatter of high heels. She smiled graciously at everyone and slid onto the bench beside Carolyn. Once seated, Emilia beamed and waved a lace handkerchief at me. Carolyn sat rigidly with her eyes closed, looking like the world was about to end. Emilia patted Carolyn's leg and waved again at me.

"Miss Cole," Attorney Corazón said, "Would you like me to repeat the question?"

"No. It's all right. I —"

Emilia jumped to her feet. "Your Honour, Your Honour," she chirped merrily. "You cannot allow my friend to answer any more questions. Look at her! She is going to faint. She is whiter than her suit."

The judge raised his chin from his hands, gathered up his notes, mumbled something, and left. By the time everyone jumped to their feet, he had disappeared through a door in the wall.

Emilia rushed forward to the witness box. "Congratulations, Kathie! You are a mother now," she said, dabbing at the perspiration that beaded my face. The young lawyers filed out, smiling and shaking their heads.

"What do you mean?" I asked Emilia. "Nobody said anything. The judge just left. When did he say I'm a mother?"

"It was all settled early this morning, Kathie. Where do you think I have been? Yes, yes, I was having breakfast with the judge. He understood and agreed to everything before you arrived already. You see? I told you not to worry. No lies, just as you wanted it. And now come. We will call for your daughter and we will all have a celebration lunch at the Manila Hotel."

Even Attorney Corazón looked pleased as she gathered up her things and stuffed them into her briefcase. I was still clinging to the wooden rail of the witness box when Carolyn threw her arms around me.

"Do you think that's really all there is?" I asked her, wondering if the judge had rushed out to the bathroom and might soon return to find us gone. "I didn't hear anybody say anything. Doesn't something have to be on record?"

"Shh! By now it likely is," Carolyn said. "Come on, let's celebrate. We're going to take Miguela home with us."

Emilia made Bert stop at a pay phone to tell Ethel to dress the baby and deliver her to the Manila Hotel. I was beginning to feel the happiness and relief that should have flooded over me the instant the judge left the room. But I was still getting my head around the fact that while I had been sweating bullets about truth and integrity, Emilia had won my daughter over a plate of scrambled eggs most likely seasoned with one-hundred-peso notes. By the time we reached the hotel, I had caught the mood of everyone else in the car. It didn't matter how or why Miguela was mine, as long as she was.

Emilia wouldn't let us wait for the baby in the hotel lobby. "It is safer if we stand on the sidewalk, Kathie. Ten days ago the lobby was bombed by terrorists. My friend's sister was killed in the blast. It is better if we spend as little time as possible there, no?"

I couldn't have agreed more and wondered about suggesting we order take-out. By and by, the car bringing my baby arrived. Mari-Miguela had been bathed and outfitted in a new, properly fitting party dress. It was very pretty. Someone had bothered to clip a tiny bow on the top of her head, but it was slipping through her fine short hair. She wore lace-frilled socks and tiny white sandals. Miguela stood on the sidewalk where she had been dropped, looking like a lost Dresden doll. Her eyes travelled from Emilia to Attorney Corazón to Carolyn to me, then searched desperately behind her for the car that was already pulling away. There wasn't one person the little girl could take comfort from, and that is why she let me step forward and gently take her hand. By the time we had reached the lobby she was sitting uncomfortably, but quietly, in my arms.

The lobby was very posh except for the section behind plywood walls. From the sounds of banging and sawing, we knew repairs were under way. Directly inside the doors were two long tables where we were instructed to stand while our handbags and belongings could be searched. I half expected a bomb to be found in my purse or under Miguela's dress, which was being lifted by a soldier. Miguela took exception to this newest stranger touching her special dress and kicked at him with a tiny sandal. Quite rightly too, I thought, as we were allowed to pass through the lobby and into the dining room. He was lucky she hadn't aimed at his nose.

Black-vested and white-gloved waiters scurried to make us comfortable; it was clear Emilia was a regular here. We were given royal treatment. "Bring a chair for the baby of my friend," Emilia instructed one young man. In no time he was back with a beautifully carved wooden high chair. Miguela was absolutely awestruck by the surroundings and attention, but especially by the chair. She was placed in it and the tray lowered over her head. I sat beside her as she examined every inch of the chair, running her fingers over its polished surface. She looked like she was witnessing a miracle. I touched the chair along with her and said something about how pretty it was, but Miguela pushed my hand away. Nevertheless, I watched the little girl, feeling very happy that she was with us and enjoying the experience.

Attorney Corazón watched, too, looking far less maternal than I. It was clear she thought children had no place in public and that this one, especially, should have been kept hidden. Her expression was one of disdain when she finally turned to Emilia and asked, "If you were going to give her a child, why didn't you give her a pretty one?"

I was appalled, but Emilia never skipped a beat. "You see, Attorney Corazón? It was the best I could do. Anyway, Kathie thinks she is beautiful — just like a mother, no? I have had the baby's head shaved already so that her hair will grow in thick, and I am having nose exercises done each evening by her ya-ya. There may be some hope."

Attorney Corazón was no thing of beauty herself, and I was offended by this whole discussion. I wondered if Miguela understood anything of the English that was being spoken around her. "There is nothing wrong with Miguela's nose," I said. "She is a beautiful little girl and I think we should change the subject right now."

Carolyn helped. She exclaimed about the wonderful "men-ooo" and asked everyone what they were having. We ordered and Emilia had a bottle of champagne brought to the table. Miguela drank pineapple juice and smacked her lips noisily at the new taste thrill. The baby was so boggled by being at a table with people that she hardly noticed that I was helping her. I gave her a bread stick and her own little curl of butter to stick it into. Things went amazingly well.

We drank and toasted our new life together and I made a small speech, thanking Emilia for everything she had done for Mari, Carolyn, and me. Miguela gave the most self-satisfied smile I had ever seen when her own plate was set in front of her. She ate with gusto and was covered in food by the time she was finished.

As the meal ended, Emilia dabbed her face daintily with her linen napkin and Attorney Corazón followed suit. Carolyn wiped the corners of her mouth and I may have, too. Miguela watched us silently, then looked down into her own lap. She had not been given a napkin and for a moment was at a loss. But not for long. In one inspired movement my new daughter twisted her leg sideways, forced her foot up under the tray, reached for her shoe, and pulled it off. She grabbed her foot, raised it to her face, unfolded the end of a much too large sock, and dabbed her mouth too, just like a lady. I thought it was very inventive and smiled proudly.

Attorney Corazón was scandalized. "What a disgrace!" she gasped, looking around to see if any of the other diners were watching. A few were. Miguela lowered her foot and allowed me to replace her shoe. When it was back on, I patted her shin and said, "Good for you." She sat heavily back in her chair, sighed contentedly, then burped, long, and loud. Attorney Corazón pushed her chair back and left, stiff-backed, to recover in the ladies' room. She was followed by gales of laughter from the rest of us.

The four of us were left at the table, co-conspirators in a mission that had taken months of planning and work. For the first time, I felt like we were all on the same side. Carolyn had initiated the contact, I had done the groundwork and sent all the required papers and documents, Emilia had pulled whatever strings were necessary in order to survive the system. And Miguela, by being there, had provided the incentive.

The singular little girl beside me stared solemnly into my face as if she was trying to decide something of monumental importance. I knew that the warmth she kept hidden behind those flat, dark eyes would shine some day. But before it could happen, Miguela had to determine that I was someone worthy of her trust.

18

"BULLSHIT BAFFLES BRAINS! IT MIGHT WORK!"

Under the impression that we had successfully finished with the due process of law, Carolyn and I had spent the rest of the day celebrating. Late that night we placed a call home and told our parents as much as we could with Emilia smiling and listening nearby. Of course, we had to leave almost everything out, but at least they learned Miguela was ours before going on their holiday the next day. Lienne was fine, they said, and getting along famously with Aunt Phyllis, so they had no worries about being away. I missed Lienne so badly it almost hurt, but with Emilia nearby the most I could say was how much I wanted to be home with the baby; which baby was up to whoever was listening.

Of course, Mother was curious about Miguela. I answered truthfully that she was very pretty, but when I hedged on the "what's she like" question, my mother sensed trouble.

"She's fine . . . sort of different," I answered. There was a pause and I rushed to fill it before Mom asked anything else. "You'll see for yourself before long. Have a good holiday and a good rest." All I heard was a small "oh" before I clicked off.

After our nice lunch I thought some ice had melted, but Miguela resented our presence in her bedroom more that night. It seemed she had had enough of us and was unwilling to put up with more. The problem continued to be the house. With it and its audience there, we would remain the enemy.

Carolyn and I decided to take her out alone the next morning so she would start getting used to us before the plane ride home. But the idea didn't sit well with Miguela. As we took her by the hand and headed down the driveway, Emilia and assorted members of family and staff watched the exodus from the compound. Miguela screamed all the way and finally threw herself down, while Emilia laughed loudly and Piña threw candies. I picked Miguela up and kept on walking, though I was beginning to think better of our expedition. The guard at the gatehouse saluted and smiled sympathetically as we passed. Miguela held her arms up to him and with her tear-stained face beseeched him to rescue her. I quickened the pace and the gate closed behind us.

Miguela's wailing continued for some time, probably causing strangers to wonder if we were abducting her. Each time one paused or made eye contact with her, she held up her arms pathetically and begged to be taken by anyone but us. Carolyn told her to stop, which had no positive effect, so we continued for blocks, no longer knowing why we were doing this or where we were going. Miguela had a high sense of drama, but eventually wore down enough to stop crying, sobbing only when a stranger came within ten feet or so. I expected a police car to roll up at any moment.

By and by we came to a small strip of stores and spent a fairly quiet hour meandering through them. Amazed by all the things she saw, Miguela finally abandoned the kidnapped routine. She observed everything with a keen eye. We found a children's clothing store and I exchanged Miguela's waif clothes for some that fit. The minute she was out of her knee length underpants and oversized sundress, she became much more amenable. This little girl liked to look nice, and she almost purred with satisfaction as she ran her fingers across the new material. The clothing was so inexpensive and sweet that Carolyn and I chose enough underwear, dresses, sleepers, and playclothes in assorted sizes to last both children for years.

After cool drinks in a café, Miguela even began to talk to me, albeit in baby Tagalog, pointing out the things she liked about her new dress. She was tired of walking and I carried her most of the way home. She spent the journey fingering the inexpensive chain around my neck.

As soon as the compound wall hove into view, she reverted to form and threw herself with wild abandon into renewed screaming. The display was truly theatrical and had the predicted result. Piña rushed halfway down the driveway and seized her poor abused little charge, popping candies and no doubt offering bribes of every description. But I had seen all I needed to see and was not nearly so worried about travelling with Miguela after this excursion.

As we entered the house, Emilia informed us that it was good we had come back now, because we had an appointment at the solicitor general's office in Metro Manila.

"Why?" I asked.

"You must be interviewed and accepted as a suitable parent before the clerk will sign the judge's adoption order and place it on file. You are not really legal yet, you see, Kathie? I cannot go with you, but Bert will stop and pick up Attorney Corazón just in case there is any trouble."

"Trouble? Why would there be trouble?"

"You see? There have been some problems lately with foreign adoptions and the rules are getting much stricter, already. There is no need to worry, but take this just in case."

Emilia produced another beautiful tin of biscuits with a bow containing money. I began to wonder if there was a store that specialized in bribe biscuits with tins sized to fit the favour being sought. I imagined shelves laden with rolled vanilla wafers for the granting of taxi licences, sesame honey crisps for adoptions or annulments, and chocolate-dipped macadamia dainties for stays of execution.

Carolyn looked dubious. "Emilia, surely you don't mean we should give money to someone from the solicitor general's office. Don't you think that's going a bit too far?"

I was glad Carolyn said it, because if I had, I would have been written off as hysterical again. Emilia took her seriously and considered the question carefully, tilting her head and examining the box. "You may be right, Carolyn. I doubt it, however. Still, if you think we are ill-advised, it is up to you. I, personally, would risk the gift. It is your decision." With that, Emilia put the tin down and hurried off to her office, only stopping long enough to say it was a good thing we had bought Miguela a new dress because she was required to be with us for the interview.

Saintly Bert was summoned again and Miguela, clutching her bottle of corn syrup, was thrust screaming and struggling into my arms. This time she fought hard, kicking and hitting as we drove through the gates. Once out, Bert stopped the car and very gently lifted her over the seat and sat her beside him in the front. He firmly told her something in Tagalog and Miguela was silent except for the involuntary hiccoughs that last long after hysterical crying bouts. She twisted around and fixed us with a look of evil intent, all the while sucking on her bottle and rotting out whatever stubs of teeth still remained. By the time we were at Attorney Corazón's home, she was asleep.

Attorney Corazón was none too happy to see Miguela out in public again, but since she was sleeping, there was very little to criticize. She climbed into the backseat with Carolyn and me and said nothing during the rest of the journey. When Bert stopped the car and indicated we should get out, I lifted Miguela as carefully as I could, trying not to wake her. She stirred and made a small noise, but settled on my shoulder and continued napping. Even at rest, her tiny body was tense.

We didn't have to wait long before we were asked to step inside. Behind a polished wooden desk sat a diminutive and very smartly dressed woman in her early forties, whom Attorney Corazón addressed as "Your Honour." We were asked to take a seat. The woman sized my sleeping child and me up immediately. She seemed to be waiting for something, as what I took to be an encouraging smile spread across her face. I returned the smile, pleased that she was surely getting a better impression of Miguela's and my relationship than if she had been walking with us earlier in the day. Attorney Corazón shuffled papers from her briefcase trying to fill what was beginning to feel like a long wait for something to begin. The pleasant expression froze, then gradually faded from Her Honour's face. When at last she spoke, her tone was surprisingly sharp.

"What is it you think you have come here to do?" she asked.

"I came here to adopt this little girl," I explained, though I was certain the question was redundant.

"And how is it you expect you can just walk into somebody's country and remove one of their children?"

The question took me by surprise. "I didn't just expect to walk in and take her from someone," I said. "I have spent a year following all the rules and requirements of your country in order to come prepared for the hearing and legally adopt an orphan."

The woman sniffed as she examined the adoption order. "And what has this judge done about your petition? He has granted it.

Yes. Still, I must sign his grant, and you see? I will not!" Her Honour dropped the paper onto the desk as she spoke. Miguela, warm on my chest, took a long shuddering breath and settled back to sleep. My heart began to race.

Attorney Corazón looked shaken. "I'm afraid, I must protest. We have already passed the hearing stage where any objections might have been raised in court. It is highly irregular for you to intervene at this stage."

Her Honour's eyes flashed. "It is my job to intervene if I see something wrong! And why were we not notified of this hearing in time? If we had been, we most certainly would have attended."

The old lawyer produced her letter to the solicitor general's office dated in November of the previous year, as well as two small newspaper notices making my intention to adopt public. "This office was certainly notified in time. Perhaps it slipped your attention somehow."

"Why was this hearing held in a court so far away? Where are you staying?" the woman demanded of me.

I opened my mouth to respond, but Attorney Corazón cut me off and gave the fictitious address, which by now was becoming familiar. Suddenly I understood why it was best to lie about where I had been living for "six months." Emilia and Attorney Corazón hadn't overlooked a single variable as they orchestrated the adoption. If the hearing was far from the centre of town, it was very unlikely that anyone from the solicitor general's office would bother to make an effort to attend. No doubt the address I was supposed to give placed the hearing in a municipality outside of their regular territory.

Miguela stirred on my shoulder and awoke, too bewildered by her surroundings to cry. Carolyn held her arms out and to my surprise the baby squirmed off my lap and onto my sister's. Scowling, and obviously at a dead end with finding any legal loopholes for the moment, the woman changed tactics and, eyes flashing, turned on me again.

"I know what you are up to and I will not have it. You are taking this child back to make her work as a domestic. I forbid it."

My throat was beginning to ache and I fought against the tears this sensation always signals. The suggestion was so ridiculous, I had a hard time searching for words that wouldn't sound sarcastic. The last thing I wanted to do was anger this woman even further. "No, I'm not going to make her work as a domestic. Not now, not ever. I only want to give her a family and a good home to raise her in. Look at her. She's so little. If I was trying to find a slave to work in my home, I assure you I would pick a bigger one."

Miguela slid to the floor, wearing Carolyn's large pair of dark glasses. She stood in front of the huge desk and peered at the angry woman. The glasses slipped forward a little and Miguela began doing her nose exercises, as if she could develop a bridge large enough to support the glasses right then and there.

Her Honour studied the baby for quite some time. "I know what you are doing," she snapped. "You intend to take this child back to your homeland and have her life heavily insured. It has happened before. After a suitable length of time the poor child will have an accident and her mother will suddenly become a very rich lady. I cannot have you murdering our children. I will have you put in prison!"

Ever since our day at the police station, I had feared the whole exercise would end in jail. I was terrified and hardly able to respond. My voice was higher than I meant it to be. "Please, I only want to love her. Why should I go to prison for loving one of your children when no one else does?"

Unable to continue, I stopped abruptly, and Carolyn took over. She spoke about the life Miguela would have in Canada and of how we had all prepared for this baby for more than five years. She listed my references and said that I was going to save this child's life, not end it. The woman heard it all with a frozen expression.

"I will give you one more chance," she said. "You must fly home to your capital city of Ottawa and go to your Embassy there. Then you must get them to give you a letter of reciprocity stating that any Pilipino who wants could come to your country and adopt a child to take to Manila. Then you must return to my office by next Tuesday morning and produce it. If the rules are the same in both countries, I will sign your paper."

We were thunderstruck. I felt like I had landed in a fairy tale and been assigned an impossible task by the Wicked Sorceress of the East. No one could possibly accomplish such a mission. But, like the star-crossed young queen in Rumpelstiltskin, I had to perform the task or forfeit my child and my freedom. I might as well have been told to spin straw into gold.

Attorney Corazón was clearly flummoxed as she tried to herd us all out before something else happened. She thanked the woman for her time and promised I would be back with the necessary paper by Tuesday morning. Outside, I fell apart and declared I was getting on a plane, all right, but I wouldn't be coming back to spend the rest of my days in jail for attempted murder.

"Stop it," my sister said, picking up Miguela and holding her out to me. "She isn't going to put you in jail. It's all a big bluff. And what about Miguela? Are you leaving her behind?"

"Where was the gift you were to bring?" Attorney Corazón demanded. "Didn't your sponsor instruct you properly?"

I was too miserable to answer either one of them. Carolyn admitted we had chosen to leave the biscuits at home, fearing a bribe would offend someone in such a high office. For the first time since we'd met, the old woman came close to laughing. "The higher the office, the more necessary the gift. If Ferdinand Marcos himself were here, the courtesy would be expected. Since you continue to ignore good advice when it is given, I cannot be held responsible. Everything should have gone smoothly, but now we are in trouble."

By this time, Carolyn had flagged down Bert. "Please take Attorney Corazón and Miguela home," she told him. "We have to go somewhere. We'll get a taxi when we are finished." Bert looked uncertain, but closed the door behind Attorney Corazón and placed Miguela on the front seat.

"I will take them home, but I must come back for you. It is too far to go in a taxi and not very safe. Please tell me where to pick you up," Bert said.

"At the Canadian Embassy," my sister told him. "I don't know how long it will take."

"It is all right. I will find it. If I am not outside when you are finished, just wait inside the door and I will be along. It is best."

Carolyn scanned the road for a cab. "Don't worry," she said. "I know it sounds serious, but I have it figured out. Emilia has contacts and influence all over the place. Whatever she gets us into, she can get us out of. And if it costs money, it's no big deal for her. She will never let you go to jail and that's that. It would be too much of a blow to her pride. This may be a challenge for her, but trust me, she'll rise to it."

I needed to believe my sister was right, and from what we had seen so far, it wasn't very difficult.

"OK," I said, "but why are we going to the Embassy? They'll never give us a letter of reciprocity because there is no such thing."

"It's time they knew what's happening. It's not a bad idea to check in with them now and tell our story, just in case."

The Embassy was in my address book, since I had written months before asking them to expedite the paperwork should the adoption go through. We hailed a taxi and arrived at the door five minutes later.

The first thing we saw as we stepped off the elevator was a large sign taped to the plate glass window: *No bribes or gifts will be accepted by any staff member of the Canadian Embassy.*

We must have looked frightened, because we were immediately taken into an office. The woman who heard our story shook her head and nodded at all the appropriate times and agreed it was good we had come now. "I'd like to be able to give you a letter," she stated, "but I can't. In truth, no Pilipino couple, let alone a single person, could arrive in Canada and adopt a baby to take back with them. You know, probably better than I do, there aren't enough children available for adoption by Canadian citizens. That's why you're here, right? I'm afraid we're stuck on that point. The ambassador is away right now and I cannot reach him. There's not much I can do about a letter."

"But couldn't you say something like 'a Pilipino couple abiding by, or fulfilling, the requirements of Canadian adoption regulations could adopt a child just like anyone else?" I asked. "The fact that the regulations state they can't doesn't need to come into it, really." Emilia's influence must have begun to rub off on me. I almost enjoyed the look of wonder on my sister's face.

The woman blinked in surprise. "Oh, I get it. Bullshit baffles brains! It might work, as long as I don't have to say anything out-and-out dishonest. I guess I can try if you want to wait. In fact, I'll have it typed on our best gold embossed letterhead. It's really quite impressive." With that, the woman left us until the wording could be properly framed and the letter typed. When she came back, she let us read the letter before sealing it in a cream-coloured linen envelope. It was a masterpiece: just the right mix of formal language and legalese.

"If you do manage to get the order signed on Tuesday, come back here early on Wednesday with a copy. We'll need it before we can give you the baby's travelling documents. You won't have any more time than you need, if you're leaving the next Saturday. And try not to worry. She can't just trump up an imaginary murder plot and make it stick. What did you do, anyway, forget to take her a gift?"

I nodded, feeling foolish for the millionth time. The woman smiled knowingly and shook her head. "Good luck," she called, as we headed for the elevator with our precious letter.

We stood waiting in the sweltering heat for Bert to battle his way back through the traffic. We were almost at the melting point when the familiar black car pulled up. I slumped in the backseat and waited for the air conditioner to do its magic, but nothing happened.

"I'm sorry," Bert said. "It has stopped working. I will have to take it to the garage tomorrow." Carolyn and I opened our windows and tried to catch some breeze as we inched our way through the bedlam.

The boulevard was wide and crammed with a colourful assortment of steaming, fuming vehicles. I turned my head in Carolyn's direction to assess how the Pope's Wall was coming along. It was lengthening, but I could still see a yet-to-be-concealed street where children were sifting through a high pile of refuse and rubbish, looking for something, anything, worth a few pesos or perhaps worth eating. Hang on, I thought. In a few days the First Lady will pay you money to paint pretty pictures on a wall that will hide your misery.

It must have been my unholy thoughts, because at that moment something hit me hard. There was a sudden pain at my throat and the back of my neck. For some reason I thought a large bird must have come in through the window and smashed itself against me. I looked down into my lap; there was nothing. But the fingers that had flown to my neck came away sticky with blood and I could feel more beginning to trickle down my back. Carolyn made a startled sound and Bert's head whipped around to see what was happening. The car shook as a man vaulted across the trunk and ran, dodging traffic to reach the safety of some narrower streets. In his fist I saw a flash of fake gold as the necklace that had so intrigued Miguela earlier was spirited away.

In an instant, Bert was out of the car and in hot pursuit. Carolyn and I followed as fast as we could, but by the time we caught up with Bert, the man had disappeared down an alley crisscrossed with clothes lines and laundry. Four men blocked Bert's way. More were quietly gathering behind them.

"Bert," I said, "It doesn't matter. The necklace isn't worth anything."

"I was supposed to keep you safe." Bert was breathing heavily and he never took his eyes off the men in front of him. One reached menacingly into his pocket.

"Please, it isn't worth getting hurt over," Carolyn reasoned. "He needs the necklace more than we do. Let's go to the car."

Bert began to back up step by step, but he didn't turn until we were at the intersection of the wider street. The men stood motionless and let us retreat, happy, I suppose, that their friend was safe for now.

I fully expected the car to be stripped bare when we got to it, but it was still sitting in the middle of the street with six lanes of traffic inching past it. Bert, pale and shaky, asked how I was. My throat did hurt a little when I swallowed, but it must have looked far worse than it was. The chain had cut into the side and back of my neck. At the front, four deep gouges had been made by thief's fingers.

Bert looked like a condemned man. He kept shaking his head and muttering all the way home. In English he apologized for letting us have the windows open. I tried to joke with him about at least not suffocating to death, but he failed to find any humour in the situation. His job was probably on the line.

After a tense ride, the compound gate opened and Bert pulled up with the evidence of his irresponsibility. Trying to make as little of it as possible, Carolyn and I stepped out of the car and waved to Ma who was sitting on the lawn waiting, as usual, to hear about our day. We tried to walk into Emilia's house, but Ma beckoned us to come. There was little else we could do but obey. Bert trudged at a safe distance behind. As we approached her chair, Ma's eyes focused on my neck and her smile vanished.

"My Lord in heaven! What has happened?"

"Nothing at all, really," I answered. "The air conditioning broke down in the car. Bert warned us not to open the windows, but we were so hot we stupidly ignored him. Then from out of the blue a man snatched the necklace I was wearing and ran. Bert was very brave. He chased the fellow into a narrow street, but some rough-looking men stopped him from going any farther. One pulled a knife and there was simply nothing Bert could do. At that point he made us go back to the car."

Ma's eyes darted approvingly to Bert. "You did all you could do, Bert. You must go home now and rest. We will see you tomorrow."

Once Bert was excused Ma examined my neck with a trained eye. Her old hands prodded gently as she assessed the situation.

"Honestly, it's just a scratch. I'm absolutely fine," I protested.

"Hush, child," Ma said. "You never know. He might have had rabies. Millie! Millie! Bring my medical bag immediately!"

Millie came running with a black doctor's bag and Ma immediately began applying every disinfectant ever invented. As she did, she told us not to worry, she had been a physician before her retirement. The last patch of gauze was being taped in place when Emilia returned home and hurried over to see what the excitement was all about. Carolyn did her best to diffuse the whole thing, but it was pointless.

"Oh my goodness!" Emilia clutched at her heart. "Mama! She must have her tetanus shot. She might well have lockjaw."

"Lockjaw, rabies, it doesn't really matter," I mumbled. "On Tuesday I'm going to be executed anyway." No one but Carolyn heard or understood.

"Where was Bert? Where is he now?" Emilia demanded.

"Bert was quite heroic, Emilia. I sent him home," Ma said. "You would do well to calm down or your blood pressure will rise. You have always been the excitable one. Look how calm Kathie is, and she is the one who was attacked." This small chastisement made my day.

"Well, this is a disgrace!" Emilia continued, ignoring her mother's advice. "I must phone the First Lady and tell her how our visitors have been treated. She must do something."

"You know Imelda Marcos?" Carolyn asked.

"Of course. She must come and apologize herself."

This was too much. I, the injured party, was having no part of a private audience with Imelda Marcos. I could just imagine what kind of interest she might take in our mission. I refused to let Emilia call her.

"Then we must replace the chain. What carat was it, Kathie, eighteen or twenty-four?"

How humiliating. It wasn't even close to being gold washed. I hesitated, which only convinced Emilia the damned thing was solid. "I really don't want you to replace the necklace, Emilia," I said. "It had no real value or even any sentimental value. I would rather the man had it anyway. I'm afraid he'll be very upset when he finds out it's not worth anything."

"It will serve him right," Ma said. "Now tell me, how was your day before this incident? Did your appointment go well?"

Elana joined us and we all sat down to drink the sodas that appeared. Ma's medical bag was removed and Carolyn related the whole story of meeting with the miserable clerk of the court. Emilia was vindicated, but not very happy.

"You see, Carolyn? I know what is best in these matters. Oh

well. It is not impossible, I suppose, though now it will be much more difficult. I will have to do some investigating on my own this evening and come with you already on Tuesday. Try not to concern yourselves for now. Tomorrow we must enjoy the day I have planned."

As soon as the drinks and merienda were finished, Emilia ushered us back to her house and launched into her one-woman investigation. Well into the night, she came to our room, victorious and flushed with success. "I have done it! I discovered I have a friend who went to school with the woman's cousin. I know the home town of her husband and several of her relatives. One of them told me what her favourite perfume is. I will send Baby shopping for it tomorrow and I will go prepared to discuss her family and friends on Tuesday. All will be well, but you must remember to take the biscuits next time, OK?"

We both agreed that we now fully understood the wisdom in biscuits.

"What did I tell you?" Carolyn asked, when the door closed behind her. "There is no stopping this woman, not even if she has to go to the First Lady. It's all going to work out, Kath. We've almost made it through the first week."

"It's been one hell of a long five days," I said. I peeled the gauze off and examined my neck in the mirror. Ma's tinctures made it look as though Jack the Ripper were alive and well, but the wounds under the stains weren't deep. Surely things couldn't get any more bizarre. Surely if Santo Niño was watching, he would spare me from rabies and lockjaw.

19

"EXPECT A MIRACLE"

The weekend cemented our relationship with the family. It started on Friday with a tour of Buti's pig farm. This was one of his many expensive hobbies and we were confirmed in our feeling that Buti did nothing by half measures. Before the day was over we had learned much about the white pigs he imported from Europe. They were kept in more hygienic conditions than most people. The wheels of the car were run through a pool of disinfectant and our shoes were wrapped in green booties before we could contaminate the ground. Each sow had her own special attendant. Awards were given to the worker who could tend the largest litter of piglets with the fewest fatalities. The entire staff would be treated to an annual holiday in the country if the farm met its quota of live births. These were definitely state-of-the-art pigs who were treated to the best — while in the land of the living. Still, I never felt quite the same about our breakfast pork and sausages after the tour.

Saturday's excursion to Elana's fish farm was an all-day affair.

Bert drove the minibus loaded with eight of us, including Miguela, out to the beautiful country estate. Elana's helpers netted huge quantities of shrimp and cooked them for our lunch. On the return trip, we were shown one of the family restaurants and told proudly that this particular chain of eateries had been responsible for the slaughter of fourteen thousand chickens in one go. Every last one of them had been consumed the year before on St. Valentine's Day. This year, plans were afoot to reduce the poultry population by a record sixteen thousand. Chicago's Valentine's Day Massacre paled in comparison. With a bit of luck we would miss the festivities.

After a chicken merienda and folk dance floor show, Carolyn and I were taken to Bataan and shown the impressive memorial and museum there. The faces of those who died on the Death March during the Japanese occupation were permanently etched in my memory as we walked silently through. Ma had no desire to revisit the past and waited in the car. As a young woman she had been separated from her husband and forced by the Japanese to march with the thousands of others. Along the way she was beaten with rifle butts and threatened with death as she fell and rose and staggered and fell again. She finally crawled, unseen, into some underbrush where she gave birth to her first two children, twin boys, one of whom was stillborn. Ma told us her story under a sparkling windswept sky that seemed to deny the existence of such cruelty. When she described covering her dead infant and leaving him without even a marker, she wept.

All the way home, sun-drenched and weary, Miguela sat on my knee. Together we counted six peanuts over and over as she dropped them into my glasses case and spilled them out again. Feeling very close, I kissed her head and told her she was a wonderful little girl. She was slightly taken aback by this show of affection, but only momentarily. She looked into my face and beamed a rare, gummy smile, then urinated in my lap.

On Sunday, we survived our second family reunion. By now most of the relatives had learned of our day in court and congratulated us heartily. My neck, a colourful blend of purple, green, and yellow bruises, sparked shock and indignation in one and all. I was beginning to feel like a local folk hero by the time the story of the vicious attack had been passed along and magnified with each telling. We visited Pa again and told him our news. Carolyn and I, veterans of an entire week with this family, handled the day with much greater ease than before.

By evening, Emilia's own personal numerologist arrived. Oscar was obviously a man held in high esteem by the family. He greeted us pleasantly from behind thick-lensed glasses, then settled in for a night of calling upon and analyzing all the spiritual advice he could summon. Elana learned this would not be a good week to sell her oil well on Mindoro Island and Emilia was told that Wednesday would be the day to announce her funding of the fresh water well in the home village of her esposo. Buti's pig farm was predicted to succeed again this year, but Elana was told to change her motto for the fish farm to "Expect a Miracle." I was advised in no uncertain terms to think of something else to call the baby I was adopting. The total of the letter values found in each of our names was ominously even, indicating that Miguela and I were not only stubborn, but too evenly matched. "You will argue to your graves" was the sage counsel I blithely ignored that night. It was all like a game of Ouija played on a summer evening at the cottage. Still, we only half smiled at the serious predictions from the odd man who spoke with such conviction.

On Monday I sat at the breakfast table with Carolyn and Emilia trying not to think about our appointment with the court clerk the next day. It was rather like trying to forget about an impending root canal procedure. Mama and Elana strolled in to join us, now that we were all "like sisters." The chatter was happy, the balut plentiful, the ambience gentle, when Emilia suddenly asked the question that had obviously been puzzling her for days.

"You know, Carolyn, as I have said, you and Kathie remind me of Elana and myself. Whenever we go on our shopping sprees to Hong Kong, we have a wonderful time, giggling like carefree children. Yes, yes, we are very much alike. You and I are the bold ones and Elana and Kathie the timid ones. But I have been curious to know what it was you and your sister were laughing at the night we greeted you at the airport."

Carolyn and I exchanged glances. We had not seen little Wang Wang or big Pete since our arrival, so it seemed safe enough to tell. Carolyn launched into the story of our tiring trip and how I was hoping to see Miguela at the airport when we landed. "She thought Wang Wang was the baby, and then when she turned him around she got a shock, that's all."

Emilia and Ma immediately burst into hysterics. Elana, far more sympathetic than Emilia, and certain she would have suffered heart failure, crossed herself quickly before the laughter overtook her.

Gasping and fluttering and dabbing with her hankie, Emilia immediately started spreading the news. "Kathie thought Wang Wang was the baby! Buti! She thought Wang Wang was Mari. Now that would be a homely child."

Buti smiled quietly. "You see, he wasn't the baby, but he is something of a celebrity here. Wang Wang is a movie star, yes. And he is a favourite of the First Lady who sponsors him and looks after his well-being. She has hired Pete as his bodyguard. Did Wang Wang show you his little silver gun? That was ordered especially for him by Imelda Marcos and it fires real bullets. He is a very good sharpshooter."

"But why was he jumping all over my luggage?" I asked.

Emilia cut in. "You see? I asked him to cause a distraction in case you were bringing in gifts or anything you didn't want looked at in your bags. I was right. You had presents and not one of your suitcases was opened.

"Good idea," I said weakly.

But Buti wasn't finished. "The First Lady has had a dog suit made for him. It is really very realistic."

"A dog suit?"

"Yes. Wang Wang is a member of the SWAT team. The suit is used in case of highjackings. You see? Wang Wang could climb a rope or somehow enter a plane and the highjackers would think he is a dog."

It was our turn to sputter. "You must be kidding! Why would any self-respecting highjacker let a rope-climbing dog with a zipper up its back onto the plane?" By now even Buti was wiping his eyes and helpless in his chair.

It wasn't five minutes before all inhabitants and helpers in the compound had heard of my faux pas. Emilia, for once, appreciated my viewpoint and admitted that she would never have been able to carry the rest of the night off. She ended by saying how very odd I must have thought they all were.

"Oh, not really," I said, still wondering exactly how good a dog suit could look on a midget, even if he was a very fine movie actor.

◄○►

Emilia had obviously decided to leave nothing else up to fate — or to Carolyn and me. One of her cousins was a travel agent and had prepared Miguela's passport documents. We went off to a photo studio to have the baby's picture taken. Miguela had wakened up very cranky and completely unwilling to be with any of us, especially Emilia, whom she obviously disliked more than anyone. I was very disappointed that she resisted me after the weekend we'd had. This little girl didn't know how to build a relationship. She lived only for comfort in the present. What had gone on before was always wiped away by a night's sleep.

At the studio, Miguela stood on a high stool, which gave her no choice but to stay still. But that didn't stop her from crying and turning her face away from the camera. The photographer finally coaxed her to look in his direction and the picture that resulted had to do. Frozen there in black and white, she looked like a member of a street gang.

Photos and forms in hand, off we rushed to have the passport assembled and signed. When we reached the passport office a long line of people were ahead of us. Hundreds of men, women, and children had taken positions on the sidewalk and had settled as comfortably as possible to wait, possibly days, to reach the head of the line. Those who were lucky or smart enough had brought an assortment of chairs and blankets. Everyone, it seemed, had packed a merienda or two.

Emilia was not accustomed to waiting and obviously had no intention of doing so. Shamelessly, she produced another one hundred pesos from her bag and tapped the shoulder of the man at the end of the line. Gesturing and speaking loudly, she instructed him to pass the money forward. With blank faces, people farther up the line received the money and gave it to someone ahead. I couldn't believe the willingness with which they all participated in allowing themselves to be moved back, even by one turn, after the wait they had already endured. In Toronto, we would have been bludgeoned to death for trying this. Here, if you had the money, you also had the understanding of those you were cheating. They would do the same if they could.

Days earlier, I had begun to be uneasy about the mounting total of all this bribe money. Emilia and I understood from the start that the legal fees, baby's care, and adoption expenses were my responsibility. I had been told how much cash to bring and I had it carefully stashed away in our room. By now I was afraid I would not have enough.

The bill must have reached its destination because about ten minutes later a paper was passed back to us by the same method. On it were instructions to come to the head of the line and make ourselves known. Ashamed of what we were doing, I lowered my eyes as we walked past everyone on the way up to the window. Emilia waved the paper and immediately the person behind an iron grill gave the signal to open the door to us. It didn't take too long to get Miguela's passport completed. We were one step closer to boarding the aircraft on Saturday morning.

Bert drove us home and we sat with windows tightly closed, the newly repaired "air con" blasting and Emilia chattering incessantly about how much harder it was these days to accomplish an adoption. "I think in all honesty, for the sake of my blood pressure, Mari will be the last baby I am giving away. The authorities are altogether too nervous now — ever since the child was murdered in Australia."

Emilia spoke as if a dead baby was no real cause for concern. I could see why the authorities wanted assurances that adopted orphans would be properly cared for abroad. But remembering Her Honour, I wouldn't have said she looked nervous so much as downright accusatory.

To dispel the concern surrounding my interview in the morning, I reached into my purse and pulled out Miguela's brand new passport. Miguela craned her neck to see, too. I gave her the small booklet to hold. When she saw herself inside, she lifted the page to her mouth and kissed it. My throat tightened and my eyes filled. Miguela had no idea of the significance of the document she held, but I did, and I was thankful that Emilia had lasted long enough in the baby business to work on this one last adoption. And since I personally was not planning a murder, I hoped that the authorities would not be too "nervous" when we turned up the next day.

That evening we had been invited to dinner by Malaya's parents. Emilia told us to dress in our best, because the restaurant we were going to was very exclusive. Also, she advised, there would be ballroom dancing after the meal. For me, both pieces of news were a huge problem. I delved into the clothes cupboard, knowing there was nothing suitable in it, but hoping Elana's new fish slogan, "Expect a Miracle" had swum into my wardrobe and provided me with an appropriate ball gown. All I came up with was Mother's frilled nylon nightgown-dress. At least I hadn't slept in it yet.

"I can't wear this," I told my sister, holding up the unattractive confection. She, at least, had a dress that looked like a dress.

"You have to. You can't wear your mother outfit. You'd die in the heat and look like you'd just come from the office. You definitely can't foxtrot in it."

That was the other difficulty. I couldn't foxtrot in anything. I can sing in time, and I can play the piano and guitar with rhythm. I can hear a beat, tap it out, and enjoy it, but I cannot make my body move to it. In fact, I have never been able to repeat anything but the simplest waltz step twice in a row without a total body spasm.

Part of the problem was a history of too many bad experiences on the dance floor. Mostly I just maimed my partners and left it at that. But some have damaged me a little, too. I have danced with men so drunk, they had to be held up. I danced with one who cried the whole time because he was "touched" to be with me. And I was repeatedly mortified by one in particular, who found dancing with me uncontrollably exhilarating. He always ended up circling me with his arms crooked, doing a turkey strut, while he whooped like a Hollywood Indian on the warpath. With him, I just gave up and stood still until the music ended, but he never seemed to notice.

I couldn't safely predict what would happen to me or anyone else when I took to the floor. Tonight, dressed in a nightgown at the exclusive Madrid Restaurant, I was going to have another dreaded opportunity to find out.

At the appointed hour Emilia, Carolyn, and I stepped out of the freshly polished Mercedes and into another world. Though Buti had been invited, he had declined. Attorney and Mrs. Mendoza met us inside. Mrs. M. wore a glittering dress, her husband a tux. I looked down at my own dowdy frock and to my horror saw it curling from the bottom up as it tried to cope with the humidity change from the coolness of the car to the moist hot air outside. I tried to smooth it back down, but it was no use. The thing had assumed a life of its own. Our hosts politely pretended not to notice and led the way into the dining room.

Attorney Mendoza was very well known to the head waiter and we were fussed over a great deal. A pair of white gloves held one of the gilt-carved chairs for me, and I sat, grateful to have the curly part of myself hidden by the table. Malaya's parents were charming and easy to talk to. They were both extremely interested in how my relationship with Miguela was developing and seemed pleased to have been instrumental in putting Emilia and me together.

During the course of the meal, which I was trying to drag out forever, we learned of Attorney Mendoza's passion for the dance. He and his wife had taken numerous courses in ballroom dancing and regularly took holiday dance cruises. By the time the crème caramel was served, I was definitely dreading the rest of the evening.

The inevitable could not be postponed. The band tuned up and began to play. Fortunately the first number was a fairly simple waltz, just about the only thing I had a snowball's chance of managing. To my dismay, the gallant Attorney, with four women to choose from, picked me as his first partner. My sister smiled demurely as we stepped onto the floor. But then something wonderful happened. I did not tread on any toes for the first few awkward bars. Bit by bit, I began to dance, really dance, in the arms of an expert. Of course, he was a few inches shorter than I, but we were as smooth as butter as we circled the floor. By degrees I could feel each muscle begin to relax in turn until my hips and knees actually felt loose. Must be the wine, I thought as I dipped a little to try it out. Before I knew it, the first dance was over and I was safe, sitting back at the table flushed with success.

Carolyn didn't fare as well. She had been spotted earlier from across the room by a bald, squat man who came over to be introduced. Attorney Mendoza knew him well and introduced us to him, pointing out that he was a general in the army. From snippets of conversation, Carolyn and I deduced that Emilia and Attorney Mendoza sat on opposite sides of the political fence. They both alluded to various situations in the government, but it was clear that for now, Emilia was fairly sympathetic to the Marcos regime, while Malaya's father was not. Perhaps this was why Buti had bowed out. In a country where poverty was rampant, those with money and influence had to be cautious — or ready to change sides at a moment's notice.

The general was now back at the table to persuade my sister to dance. When she stood up, she towered over him, but allowed herself to be led to the floor. The general turned into a veritable Fred Astaire, as long as you could forget his build. Dancing was obviously his life and he clutched Carolyn so tightly that his head was nestled somewhere in her chest. His grin, like Miguela's, was completely toothless, but not nearly as cute. They danced a tango like no tango has ever been danced before. Carolyn tried hard not to crush her partner to death as he flipped her back and forth in a passionate, wild dance. Once her eyes met mine and we were both finished. Luckily the general was very happy and took our mirth as a good sign. Emilia held her handkerchief to her mouth and giggled along with us.

By the time Attorney Mendoza had danced with Emilia and

then his wife, I was required to go only once more. Carolyn never managed to join us at the table again before the music ended. A sweating and jovial general kept her going for the rest of the evening.

Partway through the set, a house photographer appeared, just like they do onboard ships, and took our pictures for posterity. Before we left, the large glossy prints were delivered to our table as mementoes of the night I finally danced without looking like an injured seagull.

20

"I THINK WE'RE IN THE
WRONG PLACE"

Whatever Emilia did at her place of business was being neglected again this Tuesday morning. As we neared the offices of the solicitor general, she sat in the backseat between Carolyn and me clutching a large, gift-wrapped bottle of French perfume as if she couldn't rely on either of us to get it to its destination. Despite the expense of the gift, Emilia had taken care to tie the customary ribbon and money-bow over the Chanel No. 5 paper. Once more I worried that I might not have enough money to repay her when my final bill was tallied.

My letter from the Canadian Embassy was safely tucked inside my purse; I had checked it three times already, not that it would do any good if the court clerk was intent on making trouble. But now, just to be sure, I looked again. It was there.

We entered the elevator and stood waiting to be delivered to the proper floor. I was fairly composed, perhaps because I knew Emilia really did have an inside track to the presidential palace.

Even if the charge of conspiracy to murder resurfaced, it seemed unlikely that I could be tried and disposed of before Imelda's special SWAT team was mobilized. I wondered if Wang Wang would consider my rescue dangerous enough to call for his dog suit, or if he would play it cool and just stick to his gun-twirling routine. I felt like the subject of an impending international incident as Emilia, chattering gaily away, pushed open the door to announce our arrival.

The receptionist rose and opened the door to the inner sanctum. She whispered, "You may go in . . ."

. . . *said the spider to the fly*, I thought as we filed past.

Her Honour sat, dwarfed behind her huge polished desk, looking something like a child ready to play a game of grown-ups. I was pretty sure that her feet didn't reach the ground behind the modesty panel. The busyness of the day hadn't yet begun, so the only thing on the flawless wood surface was a telephone and the woman's reflection. Then, with some amusement, I noticed one of Miguela's tiny fingerprints, leftover from our first encounter, on the corner edge closest to me. If Her Honour knew it had survived three dustings, she would have had the cleaner beheaded.

Emilia stepped forward, full of confidence. "Good morning, Your Honour," she said, as she plunked the package down onto the desk. The woman's eyes flitted briefly to the gift and back up again. Then beaming one of the most benevolent smiles of all time, she stood and held her hand out to Emilia while I, in the mistaken belief that I had a role to play, fumbled in my purse for the precious letter.

"Good morning. How may I help you today?" Any trace of her former iciness had melted like a spring thaw.

Emilia jumped right in. "It is the matter of the infant my friend wishes to adopt, Your Honour. It is a simple case of your signature, that is all."

"Of course," said the sweetest woman on earth. "I remember now." She opened her side drawer and removed a pen and a folder containing the judge's order. With no further ado, she scrawled her name across the bottom of the paper and looked at me for the first time since our arrival.

"There," she said, pulling the document apart. "This copy is for you; the original will be placed on file here in Manila. I hope you enjoy your life with your child."

Open-mouthed and still holding my envelope, I took the paper and tried to follow my sister out of the room. But I was too enraged to move. I placed my hand on the corner of the desk and rubbed Miguela's fingerprint away. How dare this woman have even that much of my daughter, whose entire life had just been altered with a bottle of perfume. "Don't you even want to see the letter you sent us to get? Look, it has a gold crest on the envelope. We went to a lot of tr —"

But my sister, the human hook, had returned and was dragging me from the room. Once outside the door she let go of my arm. "What the hell's the matter with you? Are you trying to get yourself arrested? We got what we came for; let's just get out of here."

"The bitch!" I hissed. "She didn't give a good goddam about Miguela. I could be Attila the Hun for all she cares! As long as she smells nice, she can justify anything. What if I was going to have the baby murdered?"

"Well, you're not, are you? Come on! Honestly, Kath, you get the signature, and then you want to turn yourself in for further investigation! What's it to you if she's as crooked as a corkscrew? Let's just get over to the Embassy and do whatever paperwork we have to do."

Emilia was already on the street, shouting for Bert and issuing instructions to anything that moved. "I must go to my office. Bert, you will take us over to the Embassy and drop off Carolyn and

Kathie. Then take me to work and return for them. They will want to go shopping for gifts to take home for their mama and papa. Be certain to take them to the department stores. Kathie, remember to keep the windows up, yes?"

For once, we decided to be assertive and refused to let Bert return for us. "No, Emilia. You keep Bert with you. We'll do our business, go shopping, and get a taxi home. That way we can take our time."

Emilia hesitated momentarily, but agreed. After all, two full-grown women couldn't get into much trouble at their own Embassy or in a department store. We promised to be careful and strap our handbags around our necks and under our arms. Finally Bert left us, unattended, in front of the Embassy.

Once inside, we spotted our friend behind the No-Bribes-Will-Be-Accepted sign and waved our freshly signed adoption order at her.

"Congratulations," she said. "Now we have some work to do. When did you say you were planning to leave?"

"Saturday morning," I answered.

"This Saturday? We'll have to hurry. Where's the doctor's certificate?"

"What doctor's certificate?" I asked.

"You have had the child examined, haven't you? She has to be declared healthy enough to enter Canada."

"I didn't know . . ."

"Oh, Lord. What day is this? Tuesday? Maybe it can still be done, but you'll have to find a doctor willing to take you right away and hurry the test results. They take forty-eight hours to culture, which will take you to Friday. I'll do everything else you need in the meantime. You'd better get moving now."

Was there no end? Carolyn and I were handed a list of doctors who were approved by the Canadian Embassy and deemed above taking bribes to produce negative test results. Dashing for the elevator, we scanned the list for a likely looking name before it dawned on us that we didn't have Miguela with us.

"Quick! There's a phone. We'll make an appointment and then call to have the baby delivered wherever we have to go." Carolyn pulled a coin from her purse and dialled the name at the top of the column. We were immediately refused an appointment. The second call went as badly, but on the third we hit the jackpot. If we hurried over, the tests could be done in time to include in the lab's 2:00 p.m. pickup.

Millie, the cook, answered the next call. Carolyn gave the address of the doctor's office and told her we would meet her in front of the building. "Don't waste time, Millie," Carolyn instructed with enough authority that Emilia would have obeyed. "Just pick the baby up and get in the car right now."

With an appointment and a patient to go with it, Carolyn and I stood on the street waving frantically at every occupied cab in the city. Finally, a battered car rolled to a stop and we jumped in. If we had known the city better, we would have realized the address was literally within a hundred yards of where we stood; a point the driver did not appreciate in the least. We were unceremoniously dumped around the corner and, after being subjected to a string of harsh-sounding Tagalog, decided against a tip. No merienda for you, my good man.

Breathless, we entered the office, focused only on the urgency of our situation and oblivious to any of the other patients. Carolyn stood at the window separating us from the receptionist and spoke loudly enough to penetrate the glass. "Please. This is dreadfully important. We're the people who called you about ten minutes ago. We have to see the doctor as soon as possible — it's an emergency."

My rock-steady sister was finally losing it, while I, who had lost it several times prior to this, was growing calmer by the second. Now that I had the fully sanctioned adoption order and was still a free woman, I was beginning to feel invincible. We had already been through so much; nothing, least of all a stool sample, was going to stop me from getting on that plane with Miguela. After all, I had successfully dealt with poor Mr. McMann, the King of Canisters, enabling me to keep this latest hitch in perspective. Lacking such experience, Carolyn couldn't even approach my transcendental state.

The woman looked up and nodded sympathetically. "Please try to stay calm," she urged with the type of smile one saves for pathetic basket cases. "I'm sure the doctor will do his best. Just take a seat over there."

"All right," Carolyn agreed, glancing at her watch. "But we have to see him very quickly or we simply aren't going to make it."

We perched on the only two empty chairs in the waiting room. The rest were occupied by patients patiently waiting, all rather depressed-looking males, and all extremely curious by now. I tried smiling at one or two, but their intense scrutiny was more than I was in the mood to take. I knew it was too soon for Miguela to arrive, but I wanted fresh air.

"I'll go and wait outside," I told my sister, intending to pace privately on the sidewalk. As I left, Carolyn picked up one of the many pamphlets piled on the end tables and settled down to read the latest word on nutrition or breast self-examination or cardiac disease — the usual stuff one finds in doctors' offices.

Two minutes later, she came rushing out with a look of shock on her face. "Kath! Did you see any of the literature in there? Go back in and take a look. It's incredible. I'll wait out here."

I re-entered the office under the same watchful eyes of every man in the room. Sitting in Carolyn's empty chair, I casually reached for a grey folder on top of the pile. Despite its sombre appearance, it was anything but dull.

*Are you having trouble achieving or sustaining an erection?
Is flaccidity ruining your sex life? Does the size of your
penis embarrass you? Are you constantly frustrated by pre-
mature ejaculation?*

You are not alone. There is hope. We can help.

Careful to keep my head down, I crossed my legs casually and
continued to read.

* We specialize in penile implants for lasting, effective
  erections.
* Massage therapy is offered on a daily or weekly basis.
* We are experts in wet or dry mounts.
* Sexual counselling and therapy is available . . .

The man beside me had begun to shift uneasily in his chair. I
couldn't stand it; I had to look. I turned sideways and met a very
intense pair of eyes. A glance into the man's lap assured me that
one patient, at least, was on the mend. His treatment was
definitely working; in fact, it was nothing short of a miracle cure,
from what I could see. There was no indication that the doctor
was about to emerge from the treatment room in time to help
either of us, so I gathered up a few more folders and left with as
much dignity as I could muster.

Carolyn was outside waiting. "What the hell do you think?" she
asked, taking a couple of the pamphlets from me.

"I think we're in the wrong place," I answered, checking the
address we had been given. But we weren't mistaken. "Well, I'm
not going back in there alone for anything. What must they all be
thinking? What kind of emergency could two women and a baby
be having in the middle of a sex clinic?"

"How should I know? But they must figure it's terminal, from
the way we've carried on. Look, Kath, this is your kid. You'll have
to go back. I'm staying out here."

I couldn't blame her. There is a limit to what one woman, even
a sister, will do for another. Luckily, before I had to beg her not to

abandon me, a screaming Miguela was plopped just then onto the sidewalk, with little more care than one would give a sack of rice.

Miguela was growing tired of meeting us this way, and showed her displeasure openly. Carolyn and I immediately abandoned our standoff and swept Miguela, wailing and carrying on, into the clinic. There we bravely met the incredulous expressions of our fellow patients.

When the door finally opened, no one was surprised that the doctor asked us in next. With something like reverence, everyone watched us enter the treatment area. There was a collection of small cubicles inside. A strange assortment of thumps, grunts, and moans echoed from all sides. But we were taken past them into an almost normal-looking examination room where the doctor assured us we were in the correct place. He seemed mildly amused by Carolyn and me, but was extremely nice with Miguela who made it crystal clear she didn't intend to appreciate him anyway. She put up a valiant struggle for one so tiny, and knowing it wouldn't help our relationship in the least, I regretted having to help hold her still.

Ten minutes later, Carolyn and I were greatly relieved as we emerged, thanking the doctor sincerely for his help. Poor Miguela wasn't quite as grateful, but even she, seeing that we were leaving, had quieted down considerably. Moreover, the doctor assured us that he would do his best to have the test results back in time to be documented. In return, we left his patients with far more to think about than such trivial matters as size, length, and duration. We were probably the best medicine to hit the place in days.

21

"YOU WILL BE FRENCH!
KATHIE, CAN YOU SPEAK IT?"

Curiosity had finally overcome many of Emilia's friends. For the next two days a steady stream of visitors came to meet us. The gifts they brought were for the most part an excuse to see the baby and to pass judgement on her. Neither Miguela nor I appreciated the string of insensitive comments, some made in Tagalog so she could understand, and some in English for my benefit. Nose exercises were demonstrated ad nauseam, but since none of the advisors had noses of note themselves, it was difficult for me to visualize just what it was we should be striving towards.

I tried to pass Miguela a telepathic message: *only two more days and no one will make fun of you again*. But Miguela wasn't yet on my wavelength and endured the ridicule by throwing looks that literally could have killed. I tried picking her up in a gesture of support and protection but was rebuffed with a quick kick to the shin. This, of course, was met by gales of laughter. By the time the last of the gigglers had left, we were exhausted, laden with every straw place mat, coaster, and shell mobile imaginable. How we were going to become airborne with the extra cargo was beginning to concern us.

Finally, on Thursday evening, I approached Emilia about all the expenses she had incurred. I knew we had gone well above and beyond her estimated amount and I needed to know what everything had come to. Emilia waved me off, saying there was still time and not to worry about it yet. I protested, but with Emilia, when a subject was closed, it was closed. Having failed in that attempt, I had nothing to lose and tried once more to find out where Miguela had come from. I got nowhere.

—◄o►—

Buti's grey parrot woke us all bright and early on Friday morning. If nothing went wrong, this was the day we would hear about Miguela's test results.

Carolyn and I went shopping for another soft suitcase to cram with Miguela's belongings. Emilia had gotten enthusiastic and bought her three dozen pairs of underpants — all huge — as well as countless socks and six sleeper sets. Teeny had laundered all of Miguela's night diapers and clothing and those, along with the dresses we had purchased and all the gifts, filled the bag to bursting. When we finished packing as much as we could, we had to wait until we could make the fateful phone call to the doctor. Suspense was running high. More and more, I was thinking of Lienne, hoping against hope that she would remember me and accept her new sister easily.

By 1:00 p.m. we heard the words we were waiting for. It was a go. The tests were back; all were negative. The report had been made to the Embassy where the papers were now ready and waiting for us to pick up.

Before the receiver was back in its cradle, Carolyn had gathered up our purses and Emilia was summoning Bert in strident tones. In the thirteen days since our arrival, we had stopped being strangers and had become a well-oiled team. In unison, we slid onto the car's leather seats, closed all three doors with one satisfying thud, and waved to the gatehouse guard as we passed through. Why Emilia carried another biscuit tin was a mystery to me, but I didn't ask; I assumed she did it out of force of habit.

At the Embassy we had to wait while the people ahead of us went in and came out. Carolyn and I were very relaxed and unconcerned, but Emilia began to seem agitated. I wondered if she was anxious to get to her office and asked her if she wanted to leave.

"No, No! I cannot leave now, Kathie. Not with what lies ahead. But all these delays are very dangerous. We are likely not to make it in time."

Alarm bells went off. "Make what in time? We're here, they're expecting us. What's the problem?"

Emilia began to wring her handkerchief. "We have one more appointment I didn't tell you about. It is a requirement of the Philippine government before you can leave with the child. I thought we had time, but . . ."

Carolyn moved forward in her chair. "Appointment where?"

"The Department of Labour. We must go and fill out an affidavit that you are not importing the baby to use her as a domestic. I thought we would have time, you know? But now — this is very serious."

I glanced at my watch. It was 2:05. There was still some afternoon left, so Emilia's concern didn't seem well founded. Before long, we were ushered in, asked to sign numerous forms, and handed everything we would need upon entering Canada. Carolyn and I were elated and tried to express our thanks to the woman who had helped us so much. But Emilia was already in high flight. She grabbed my arm and dragged me towards the elevator, waving everyone out of our way and ranting like a mad woman about 4:00 p.m. Friday closings.

Poor Bert was told to drive on the sidewalk if necessary and did everything humanly possible to negotiate Friday afternoon traffic in Manila. Finally, we stood in another shabby elevator with Emilia shifting her weight from one foot to the other and muttering how we wouldn't make it.

"Emilia, we're here, and it's before four o'clock. What's the problem?"

"The problem, you see, Kathie, is that there is an interview. It can take anywhere from two to three hours. They will never be willing to begin it now. No, no. They will send us away to return on Monday — after your plane has left."

"Why didn't you tell us this sooner? We could have come yesterday!"

"Oh yes, but you see, I have been trying to get this appointment for days. This was the only afternoon they would see us already. I didn't say anything, because of your worrying nature. There was no point in having you nervous. I am sorry. But I think we have failed."

Even as she gave in to defeat, Emilia reached into her wallet for another bow enhancer. She added it to the one already there, making the gift that much more persuasive, but I could see by the expression on her face that this was a last-ditch effort. By the time the elevator jerked to a stop, my worrying nature had taken over.

Out of the elevator, Carolyn leaned against the wall and rubbed her forehead. "What can they possibly interview her about for two hours? Either she wants a servant or a baby. Why on earth would she import a baby to clean the house? The whole thing is ridiculous. It's just too damn bad we're not Francophones. I bet there's no one here who could interview her for two hours in French."

Emilia stared at Carolyn as if she was seeing a vision of the Holy Mother herself. "That's it! You will be French! Kathie, can you speak it?"

"Oh, please," I groaned. "Emilia, don't make me do this. The extent of my French is pathetic. *Mal de mer, mon dieu, sacre bleu.* That's about it."

"Yes, yes, it will do. It sounds very good to me. If you are required to say more, you can simply make it sound French, no?"

"No! Not with an accent like mine — and my name — it isn't even remotely French. Don't be crazy! I can't fool them."

But Emilia was already proceeding down the long corridor at a great clip. Her self-esteem was back, she was confident, it was show time. "There you go with your worrying, already," she shot back over her shoulder. "It is true, I tell you. If you can fool me, you can fool them, and you sounded very French just now. The best thing, of course, is to say nothing. Just let me do all the talking if possible and try to look as if you understand nothing. Carolyn, it was a very good idea, but you must try to look stupid, too."

My sister looked suitably dumbfounded. On the stupid part, we were both going to pass. "Don't forget *Gentille Alouette* and *la plume de ma tante*," Carolyn coached as we followed Emilia into the large, dirty waiting area.

It was a bustling, noisy place. A number of interviews were already well underway when Emilia stepped in, ready to begin. At first no one noticed her above the din, so she pumped up the volume and waved the biscuit tin tantalizingly. "Excuse me, excuse me! Is there anyone here who can help?"

A dozen or so heads turned and looked at her with disinterest, then lowered back to their tasks. Emilia put the tin down and clapped her hands loudly. Everything in the room stopped. "Is there anyone here who can speak French?"

No answer.

"Is there no one here who can help me? Can't even one of you speak French?" Not a single individual rose to the challenge, leaving Emilia free to throw herself into an Academy-Award-winning performance and increasing my chance to shine as supporting actress.

"Oh, this is most horrible," Emilia exclaimed. Out came the lace hankie to be dabbed effectively on brow and throat. "What am I going to do? I have had these two in my home for two weeks. They understand nothing. I have had to pull them to the table, push them to their beds, lead them like little children. My family is suffering, my work is ignored, my blood pressure is very dangerous, and I am going to faint."

Someone pulled a chair over and Emilia, suitably wilty, continued from a seated position. "How can an interview be done if no one can even speak to them? I tell you already, if they do not leave soon, my esposo will ask for a divorce. And then what will become of me?"

All eyes were on us, the distasteful cause of the poor woman's wrecked marriage. We stood, trying to find just the right expression to seem unaware of what Emilia was saying while being capable enough to be troublesome. Finally, someone spoke up.

"Do you think you can get them to sign this form?"

Emilia revived, a little too quickly I thought, enough to snatch the paper and bustle over to us. Two inches from my face she stared into my eyes, held up the paper, and motioned with a fountain pen. "SIGN HERE," she mouthed. "SIGN YOUR NAME."

If I had been from another planet I would have known what to do. Still, I had to look somewhat baffled for just the right length of time. It wasn't hard. Facial expressions of brainlessness and terror are very closely linked. Finally, I signed the paper and looked to Emilia for approval.

"Do you think you can get her to sit down here?" the same man asked. I allowed Emilia to guide me to the chair and sat obediently when given the hand signal.

Once at the desk, I was presented with various challenges, mostly involving my signature. I almost slipped when the man asked to see my passport and airline ticket. But Emilia jumped in. "SHOW YOUR TICKET," she said, flapping her arms like a bird to remind me I couldn't understand a thing. "YOUR AIRLINE TICKET." My days of watching *I Love Lucy* re-runs were standing me in very good stead. I gave Emilia my best imitation of Lucy Ricardo feigning innocence.

"You see? Do you see what I have been up against?" Emilia appealed to the man. "It is hopeless." With that, she grabbed my purse and produced the ticket and passport.

By this time, the man wanted us gone and sincerely wanted to spare himself the difficulty of the interview on this or any other day. "It is useless to try to ask the normal questions in this case," he said. "If you can vouch for this woman's character, we will consider our job done."

"Yes, yes. I can quite easily say she may be none too bright but she is quite harmless and appears to be honest."

"Then if you will be kind enough to fill in the necessary blanks, here, here, and here, we will be finished."

Emilia supplied the information without delay, and at exactly 3:40 p.m., twenty minutes before closing time, we had the final paper in hand. It was a miracle of timing and human ingenuity.

Emilia, much like a farmer shooing chickens, herded the two of us out. Not until we were alone in the elevator did we dare to fall upon each other, laughing and crying and bedazzled with success. "You were really very good, Kathie," Emilia praised as she wiped the tears from her eyes. "I didn't really think you could manage it, but yes, you did. We have accomplished everything and look! I even saved the biscuits! You must take them to your mama and papa. They are really very tasty."

Somehow Emilia had managed to pick up her biscuit tin on the way out and now she was waving the money at us. "And with this, we will celebrate. Come. I will treat you to some halo-halo. It is a favourite dessert here in Manila and you mustn't go home without tasting it. We are blood sisters now, the three of us. That was as good a time as I have ever had."

Bert was summoned and told to take us to a nearby café. Emilia included him in the celebration and he seemed to enjoy, far more than I, the mixture of shaved ice, coconut milk, tapioca, fruit, nuts, and syrup. Nevertheless, I choked it down like a good blood sister should. I could have eaten anything at that moment and thought it was pure heaven. Carolyn and I were going home to Lienne, and Miguela was coming with us.

The party continued well into the night. When Buti heard the news, he made a reservation at his favourite restaurant and his entire family, Ma and Elana included, dined with us in style. My nightgown was trotted out one last time. As I put it on, I thought that it was beginning to look pretty good. After all, it had taken me dancing at the Madrid Restaurant.

In bed that night no one slept. Miguela was fitful and cried out repeatedly. Even corn syrup didn't placate her. I wondered how much she understood about what would happen in the morning. Though I believed in my heart of hearts that we were her salvation, I felt pangs of guilt and worry as I watched Piña tend to her needs. And when at last they settled down to sleep, I noticed how tightly they clung to each other, as if it was their last night on this earth.

I lay awake the rest of the night, wondering about this gamble, half convinced I was Miguela's champion and half worried that I was stealing what little comfort she had in living. What if she needed someone far more experienced than I, and from her own culture at that, if she was truly going to flourish? In the end, I had to stop. With no small amount of help from dozens of people, fate had already played its part. For better or for worse, right or wrong, sane or insane, I finally had my family — till death do us part.

22

"WATCH IT, KID.
THIS IS MY MOTHER."

Our last morning was full of goodbyes. Emilia's daughters, all except one, ate with us and gave us letters and cards of farewell. Magdalene, unable to sleep all night, had written a long letter tightly sealed in an envelope "to be opened on the plane." At the table, Elana sat beside me and prayed for our safe return home and for the future of our family. She also gave me a parcel of embroidered handkerchiefs for Miguela "to wipe away her tears of joy."

I waited for an opportunity to see Emilia alone and finally it came. Suddenly, I felt close to this woman who had been such a puzzle to me at the beginning. I tried to express my gratitude — something that was impossible to put adequately into words. She waved it aside, saying how fond she was of Carolyn and me. Finally the awkward subject of money had to be addressed.

"Emilia, there isn't much time left. I brought the money you said you would need. It's here in this envelope. I know I owe you more and I will send it when I get home, I promise."

Emilia shoved the envelope back at me. "You see, Kathie, I have discussed the matter with my esposo. We are in perfect agreement. It is not necessary to give the money. We will consider the matter closed."

"No," I protested. "You have done far too much already. This was understood from the beginning. I want to at least pay back what this has cost you."

With a suddenness that surprised me, Emilia threw her arms around me and said, "It would be wrong, no? To take money from a sister. We are family now. No more talk of money."

I appealed to Buti, who stood watching. He smiled quietly and said, "Consider it Miguela's dowry. You will need it; a daughter can be an expensive item. You are only a beginner, so you must listen to me. I know, I have five of them."

I was sorely tempted to break down and tell Buti that I was catching up to him at breakneck speed, but this wasn't the time. The three of us walked towards the car. Bert stood waiting, as did the entire staff, just as they had the night we arrived. Could it only have been two weeks ago?

There was Elana, and Ma, all the children, and there, apart from everyone, was Piña, holding Miguela by the hand. I blessed Mama one last time, feeling the dangerous tightening in my throat. "Till we meet again," she said with a smile, knowing we never would.

Carolyn said her goodbyes, too. Finally, I had to go to the baby and take her. *Please don't cry*, I begged her silently, while everyone stood watching. Miguela, sensing something big, clutched at Piña and began to scream. I kneeled down to be at her level. "Come on, sweetheart. It's going to be all right." Piña, looking miserable, shoved the baby roughly at me. Miguela began to flail as I reached for her and turned quickly towards the car. Inside, her crying seemed even louder and at that moment, I hated myself as much as she did.

Emilia, determined to see us off, took her place in front and slowly we circled the drive and passed each waving hand, then made our way down to the gate. Even the guard forgot his customary salute and raised a white glove in farewell. By the time I could twist to look through the rear window, Piña had run to the sidewalk outside and stood, small and alone, with her hands hanging loosely at her sides.

Above the din, Emilia began issuing instructions. "Carolyn, I expect Kathie will be too busy to remember, so I am counting on you already. You are to give your mama and papa my regards. I know that if my papa were alive, he would have liked you very much. You must write to me, no? I want to hear of all your progresses and even your setbacks. Make sure to send pictures, too.

"Kathie, you must take this. It will drug Mari and keep her quiet on the plane. I gave it to the last baby I sent and his mother wrote to tell me it was very successful. It is a very clever idea and I recommend it, OK?"

"What is it, Emilia?" I asked, turning the brown bottle in my hand.

"It is only cough medicine, very harmless. There is codeine in it to make her sleep. You can give it freely as needed."

I stashed the clever idea in my already bulging purse, horrified at the thought of pouring codeine freely into any baby, and thanked Emilia for her thoughtfulness.

At the airport, we pulled up to the departure ramp and said goodbye to Bert. He wished us luck and touched Miguela's sweaty forehead, before getting back into the car to park it. As we turned away from him, I caught sight of two familiar figures. Wang Wang and Pete were ambling towards us. I looked at Emilia, who was all a-twinkle.

"It is my parting gift to you, Kathie. A remembrance of your first look at the baby." Emilia seemed to think this was a very funny joke and held her hankie to her mouth. "Besides," she choked, "Wang Wang could be very useful when it comes time to show your papers. Come."

With that, Emilia bustled forward and Carolyn and I followed close behind. Wang Wang fell in line and Pete hung back with the luggage, allowing the limelight to fall on his little friend. Wang Wang began to swagger as we entered through the doors and had completed the first of many acrobatic feats by the time we reached the counter. The circus was leaving town.

I was surprised to find Malaya's mother and young brother waiting to see us off. Miguela allowed herself to be held by Malaya's mom while my papers were examined. Wang Wang stopped his athletic display and stood quietly, twirling his gun, the one with real bullets. The effect was not lost on the immigration officer who cast sideways glances at him from time to time. Finally he stamped Miguela's passport, then Carolyn's, then mine and handed them back along with all the documents. The bags cleared customs and disappeared on the conveyer belt, leaving our small entourage suddenly with nothing to do but bid each other goodbye.

Miguela was handed, crying, back to me and when Emilia tried to speak to her, she turned her face into my neck and hid. One last embrace and we were through the gate, lugging an impressive amount of hand baggage. My last glimpse of Emilia was as she stood waving her hankie and smiling broadly. "*Mabuhay*, Carolyn and Kathie," she called. "Long life!" Wang Wang must have been paid, because he and Pete were already strolling away, satisfied with yet another flawless performance.

Once through the metal detector, we let Miguela walk on her own. She was still protesting, but the real crying seemed to have stopped for now. I flopped down in a chair, hardly able to believe we had gotten this far with no trouble. I waited for the announcement to board the plane like a criminal on the run, trying to look casual while on the alert, expecting to be apprehended at any moment.

Even when we were seated on the aircraft, I thought something would happen; there would be an announcement — "Would passenger Cole please make herself known . . ." Only after the doors closed and the engines roared to liftoff could I believe we were really on the first leg of our journey home.

The flight to Tokyo wasn't terribly long, but with Miguela it seemed longer. She had no seat of her own, and, not wanting to be held by either of us, she cried all the way there. Somehow we killed the three-hour wait in the terminal and changed planes.

From the start it was clear that this flight was going to be far more miserable than the first. Carolyn and I had scored bulkhead seats, which gave us extra leg room and, more importantly, a place for Miguela to stand. We were in the middle section of the plane sitting four abreast. A young couple sat beside us dandling their happy baby, a round, bald dumpling of a child. They offered sympathetic smiles in our direction as I tried to contain Miguela on my lap for the takeoff. She was full of fight again. Carolyn tried to distract her, but it was no use. We were becoming rapidly unpopular to those seated anywhere within ten rows of us.

Airborne at last, Carolyn and I grinned at each other, full of the significance of the moment. As soon as the carts came out, we would celebrate with a cold drink of something.

Finally the "fasten seat belt" sign went off. I placed Miguela on the floor in front of me, hoping she would settle down if I didn't have to hold her. Immediately, the stewardess came by. "You really should hold the baby on your lap," she instructed. "It's safer for her there."

"Just let her settle a bit first," I said. "She's been quite upset."

"Yes, I can see that," the woman sniffed. "How old is she?"

"Twenty-one months," I answered, not knowing it would have been simpler to claim she was younger.

"And how old is your baby?" the woman asked the couple beside us. Their response was greeted with a cheerful, "Oh, would you like a bassinet to put him in?"

"Could we have one, too?" I asked, certain that if Miguela could have her own little bit of space, she would settle down and maybe even sleep.

"No, you can't. Your child is too old. It wouldn't be safe."

"But my child is half the size of theirs," I remarked. "Surely if it's safe for him, it will hold my little girl."

"It doesn't matter. Twenty-one months is too old." With that the flight attendant left to find the other baby a bed. It came and was snapped securely into the wall facing us. The chubby little being sat proudly grinning at his parents, looking like a toothless Buddha with raisin eyes.

"Look," I said. "Can't you ignore the rules this once? Bring her a bed will you, please?"

The woman left and did not return until it was time to instruct me to hold Miguela again. Renewed wailing was the result of this order. Carolyn and I took turns trading our unwilling charge back and forth as we soared across the ocean.

We took turns eating, too. Miguela was totally disinterested in food, but needed a drink badly. I tried offering her some juice, which she seemed to want, but the minute it touched her mouth, she yelped and spat the liquid out. Further attempts resulted in apple juice all over the place.

The movie played and no one could hear it even with ear-phones on. Carolyn and I juggled and jiggled and sang and soothed all to no avail. Finally Miguela began to vomit, the result, I thought, of being overwrought.

I took her to the washroom and sponged her off, changed her into clean clothes, and tried to get her to calm down. Instead of returning to our seat, we paced up and down the aisle, much to the disgust of everyone trying to settle down to sleep. This twelve-hour flight was stretching into an eternity. At long last, Miguela was exhausted enough to droop on my shoulder and I went back to the seat. Carolyn spread some blankets out on the floor in front of us. Ever so gently, I put my sleeping child down and covered her. It was the first silence we'd had in four hours. I settled into my seat, put my head back, and closed my eyes.

"You cannot put the baby there." It was the voice of our friend. "What do you suggest?" I said, opening my eyes.

"You'll have to pick her up. It's against the rules for her to be on the floor."

Carolyn had had enough. "Well now, you have a choice of which rule you would like to break and which you would like to obey," she said. "Either you bring us a goddam bassinet or you pick her up and hold her all the way to Chicago, because we're not touching her again until she wakes up of her own accord."

The flight attendant brought the bed. "This is not right," she said, looking at Miguela with obvious distaste. "What's the matter with her, anyway?"

"You figure it out, lady," I said, trying unsuccessfully to lift Miguela without waking her. But this time she only cried for a few minutes before drifting back to sleep, secure in her place apart from us.

For one blessed hour we rested as well as one rests on an airplane. And then the crying started all over again. I opened my eyes and looked at Miguela. She appeared somehow different. I nudged Carolyn. "Does she look the same to you?"

"No. Good Lord. What's happening to her face?"

I didn't know, but suddenly the bottom half of the baby's face was bigger and fatter. She continued to howl bitterly and it soon became apparent that the problem was her teeth. Greyish ooze began to dribble down her chin and when I tried to wipe it gently away, the wailing was interrupted by high-pitched shrieks of pain and fear. Miguela was in serious trouble.

We pushed the help button and a different, more understanding attendant brought towels to hold against her face. Miguela allowed herself to be picked up and rocked. Any small comfort was a blessing now. She pawed at her mouth and ears, causing me to wonder if they were aching, too. Suddenly I remembered Emilia's cough medicine.

"Carolyn," I asked. "How much codeine would it take to make her comfortable enough to sleep?"

"I don't know, but it's a great idea." With considerable effort, we finally got the third spoonful into the baby's mouth and down her throat without spilling it. Sticky and upset, we spent the rest of the long, long flight keeping Miguela as quiet and pain free as possible.

Completely frazzled and definitely worse for wear, we finally arrived in Chicago for a brief stopover. Our friends, Tony and Kaye, were there to meet us and had obtained special permission to enter the in-transit waiting area so they could visit with us. Full of excitement, they waved a bouquet of flowers at us and came smiling forward. Then their jaws literally dropped. We must have looked like we had been through two weeks of hell.

Bless them, they declared the baby was . . . cute. "She really is, you know," I said. "She feels awful right now. She's had a bad time."

Kaye looked as if she might cry. "She'll be fine in no time, you'll see," she said. "She'll thrive as soon as she's home." Tony tied a helium-filled balloon to Miguela's wrist, and surprisingly, she was fascinated by it. She spent the hour tottering around in a drug-induced state watching the balloon bob above her until we were all dizzy.

"How was it? Did the hearing go smoothly?"

Despite our fatigue and worry, we had to laugh. "Smoothly! Oh, Kaye, you had to be there." We chattered like two mad women until it was time to go. I had no idea what day it was, what time it was, what year it was. I just wanted to be home with Lienne and Miguela in my own wonderful bed.

One more takeoff, one more landing. It was almost more than the baby could stand. Her face swelled even larger with each change of altitude. By the time we reached Toronto she was a limp, damp smidgeon of humanity.

I was very nervous that when we showed our papers to the officials, something would prevent us from entering the country. We were ushered into a booth and interviewed very briefly. Our papers were looked at, and everything was declared in order. All we had to do was clear customs. As we headed for the escalator to take us to the baggage claim area, a woman drew alongside us. "Here, let me help you with some of this. You look a little tired."

"Oh, thank you," I said, adjusting Miguela on my hip and allowing her to take the bag of place mats and diapers. She saw us to the carousel, put our stuff down, and said goodbye.

To our surprise, when we got to the inspection station, the same woman was behind the counter we had chosen. "Hello again," she said, but her friendly smile was gone. "Put everything up here." We lifted the bags up onto the counter. "Open them," she ordered.

I don't know what the woman was looking for, but she went through every last dirty diaper, empty baby bottle, and each pair of underwear we had with us. All our belongings were spewed on the floor and counter. Miguela was crying again and I was almost ready to join her. I looked sideways to see our neighbour Betty through the glass. As arranged, she had come to pick us up in our parents' absence. She stood waving a child's red plaid coat and a pair of leggings she had borrowed from someone.

The customs officer emptied our purses, took our camera apart, and even checked inside the diaper the baby was wearing. For one mad moment I considered offering her twenty dollars and the biscuit tin that had been saved for my parents.

Finding nothing she could arrest or even tax us for, the woman seemed disgusted. "Put everything back and get it out of here."

"Just a minute," my sister said. "You unpacked it. You pack it back up again."

I couldn't believe it. We were thirty seconds away from being through the gate and finished with our long ordeal and Carolyn was up for one last showdown.

The woman's eyes narrowed. "What did you say?"

"I said, we didn't mind you pulling everything out if you wanted to look at it, but we already packed this stuff once and we're tired. You put it back."

To my utter amazement, the woman began to fold and stuff everything back. She even did it rather neatly. When she was finished she looked up. "Now please remove your bags," she said.

I practically raced for the door and Betty's waiting arms. It was cold outside, she said, as she offered the coat and leggings for the baby. It was February 7. I had almost forgotten winter.

"How is Lienne?" I had to know.

"She's fine. Your aunt has been having a great time feeding her up. Your mother and father phoned and they're having a good time."

Betty stood looking at Miguela and began to cry. "Oh, Kath, she's so small."

"Yeah, but she's mighty," I said, shoving her feet into the warm pants. "Let's go."

Not once did Miguela cry, all the way home. She sat looking catatonic, moving nothing but her eyes. Her heavy outer clothing must have felt very strange and Miguela reacted as if it had rendered her paralysed. The cold, bare landscape that greeted her was equally strange. Where was the colour? Where were the orchids? Why had the sun fallen? I tried to talk to her, to reach her, to keep her from retreating, but it was pointless. Miguela seemed to be in a world of her own.

Twenty minutes later, we reached our street. Once out of the car, I handed Miguela to Carolyn. "You'd better carry her in," I said, hoping Lienne was too young to be jealous.

Looking up the driveway, I saw Aunt Phyllis standing at the window, holding my other precious girl. Jason and Chris were at the door waving and jumping up and down.

We hugged the boys and entered the house. My aunt still held Lienne tightly. I could see she was having trouble letting her go. The baby looked at me with an incredulous expression as a wide grin spread across her face. Aunt Phyllis put her down, and with an amazed "Da-da!" she toddled forward on chubby legs. Lienne fell into my arms, erasing my biggest fear. She had remembered.

I walked over to where Carolyn stood holding Miguela.

"Look, Lienne. I brought you a sister." I stroked Miguela's arm and Lienne reached out to touch her, fascinated to see someone the same size as she was. Miguela pulled her arm away, but studied Lienne intensely.

We put them both down on the floor and I sat between them cross-legged and holding my breath.

Lienne approached, looking friendly. Miguela stood her ground, looking unfriendly. Lienne toddled off to retrieve a toy, which was offered in a gesture of friendship. Miguela didn't understand toys or friends and refused to take it. The foam block fell to the floor. Lienne must have assumed her duty was over. She turned back to me and sat heavily on one of my bent legs to resume our reunion.

This apparently was too much for Miguela. It wasn't like she was fond of me yet, but here in this vast strange place with no flowers, I was the most familiar thing she had. Ignoring her debilitating winter wear, she lurched forward and plopped down on my other leg. There she sat, glaring at Lienne, the picture of jealous indignation. And the message went out! "Watch it, kid. This is *my* mother."

My aunt threw back her head and laughed her warm, rolling laugh. I can still hear it to this day. And in a voice that was at the same time hers and my mother's and grandmother's, she said, "Oh, my dear, what have you done? I tell you, girl, you're for it now." Wiping her eyes, she bustled out to the kitchen. "It looks like you could both use some tea. I'll get it."

In no time the tray arrived, but it didn't have tea on it and it wasn't carried by my aunt. Tall glasses of bubbling champagne sparkled no more brightly than my mother's eyes behind them. Dad followed, beaming, eager to catch a first glimpse of his newest grandchild.

Our journey, at last, was over. From fields so far away, we had all finally come home.

EPILOGUE

Many stories of perseverance are over at the end of a book. The patient recovers or dies, the marriage survives or fails, the climber freezes to death or reaches the mountaintop. The end of this story was, of course, our beginning. In some ways this ending is literally where the girls, and I, are born. And I remember it all, as I promised I would, with shining clarity.

Miguela, after a very hard and taxing start, did take hold. Her teeth — four extractions, eleven cavities, and six crowns later — finally stopped torturing her. Little by little, she had to accept the fact that the sugar was gone and that food was interesting. She gained weight, though not until I had been embarrassed many times by strangers' unkind comparisons on the street. "What's the matter? Don't you feed that one?"

The person she was hardest on, and learned the most from in those early days, was her sister. Miguela's strong nature held her together through the first difficult months and held her back through many more. But by September of that year, a full seven months after her landing, she attempted to give her first kiss. It was an awkward affair, a shy brushing of the lips against a cheek with a loud smack after contact was severed, but the cheek was mine, and it was a red-letter day. I wrote it in her book, know-ing that once she truly felt the beginnings of affection stir within her, she would be hungry for more.

Lienne continued to thrive despite some frightening setbacks. But on the morning of her sister's dental surgery, she almost died. I had gone in to wake her a little earlier than usual. She was drowsy and after being dressed, drifted back to sleep. I got Miguela ready and returned to Lienne. She smiled sleepily and closed her eyes again. By the third attempt to rouse my normally early riser, I was concerned.

Picking up both children, I ran for the car. At the house, Mom tried to reassure me. "She's just tired. Go on now and take care of Miguela. I'll look after Lienne." But as we were on our way out the door, Carolyn arrived to wish Miguela well.

"Come on," she said after one look at Lienne. "We'll all go."

The drive to Sick Children's Hospital was terrifying. Morning traffic was slow and Lienne was as floppy as a rag doll in Carolyn's arms. At one point I was driving with the horn on and praying for a police car, while Carolyn checked to see if Lienne was still breathing.

At the hospital Lienne received immediate attention. So did I. "Did you shake her? Did you give her alcohol? Where were you yesterday? Could she have gotten into poison? Are you sure you didn't give her alcohol — not even one sip of beer?"

Of course, I understood the questions were necessary and I was telling the truth with every "no" I uttered. Still, I could see doubt on the faces around us and began to panic. Time was passing. I was the only one who knew for certain this line of questioning was a dead end.

Blood was taken, a spinal tap done. Then, as we waited for the results, a nurse came in and took Miguela away for her appointment with the dental surgeon. Poor Miguela looked startled as she disappeared with Carolyn following close behind. I had promised her I would be with her.

For a moment I was alone with Lienne. "Don't go away," I

begged as I stroked her fingers. "Please, don't leave me after all this."

Then we were being rushed down the hall for a CAT scan when the doctor called us back. Blood work showed that Lienne was hypoglycaemic. Before long, she was being treated and showing signs of rapid recovery.

That day, I ran from floor to floor to check both of my babies and to let them know I was there. "How many kids do you have in here?" one bewildered nurse asked, as I flew past on a mad dash to the elevator.

"Only two," I called back. "It seems like twenty."

That first year was anything but dull.

—◦—

People tend to think that when your children are adopted, you are extremely objective about them, and that they have a right to know everything and say anything they like. Until they were eight or nine, people would cross a road to ask questions about the children as if they were blind and deaf. Most of the questions, though somewhat insensitive, were mundane: "Are they twins?" "Where are they from?" "How long have you had them?" But some rose to new heights: "Oh my God, they're adorable — which one do you prefer?" and my all-time favourite, uttered with copious amounts of sympathy, "Ahhh . . . Is their mother dead?"

My family got used to being stared at in restaurants and, for the most part, smiled back into kind faces. We learned to ignore the stunned or disapproving ones, though a few times I was inspired to rise and remind people that their dinner was getting cold. Once, none too subtly, I told a man he was entitled to his opinion, but likewise we were entitled to a nice family night out. I didn't care if he thought the "Asian hordes were taking over" as long as he thought it in silence, so that my children didn't have to ask: "Why doesn't that man like us? Is it because we forgot our party shoes?"

It didn't take long for the girls to stop feeling new to me, and given the makeup of the rest of our family, it didn't take long for other homogeneous units to start looking odd to us. But one night, after lagging behind to help Lienne with the buttons on her coat, I was forced to reassess that perception. As we hurried to catch up to my parents, Carolyn and Chris, Jason, and Miguela, I heard the waitress and the hostess deep in conversation. "Did you see the group of people that just left? That was the strangest bunch I've ever seen. They had two of everything, and everybody was calling somebody else Mom!" She had a point.

—◄o►—

At nearly four, my children, like everyone else's, were ready to be registered for junior kindergarten. The interview and assessment, conducted by a humourless school nurse, were a nightmare. Lienne, never at a loss for anything, was the one I pushed forward first. Miguela still viewed any stranger with a great deal of suspicion, sometimes close to hostility.

"What's your mommy's name, dear?" Easy. Lienne knew that one.

"Mommy," she answered.

"Mommy what, Lee-Anne?"

"Mommy Cole."

"Oh," the nurse observed, noting the simplistic answer on her form. "And what's your daddy's name?"

Lienne paused only a second. If coming to this school meant she was supposed to have a daddy, then no sweat — she'd have one. "Mr. Heinrich," she announced proudly.

The nurse looked startled, but not nearly as much as our apartment superintendent would have, had he been there to hear his paternity proclaimed. I began to feel uneasy.

"How old are you, dear?"

"Three and a half, but I don't got my moustache yet." Oh, Lord. Lienne was about to report on the state of her physical development.

"Your what, dear?" asked the lady, bending close to hear better.

Lienne began pointing at her crotch. "My moustache. I don't got one yet. It's coming later."

I pretended a trip to the bathroom was in order and hoped the woman was clever enough to move along to other things. When we got back, she was looking at Miguela, the way one might observe a potato beetle.

"Have the children been to the dentist yet?" she asked.

For some reason, known to her alone, Miguela chose that moment to stop scowling and smile one of her rare beatific smiles, revealing the four-tooth gap that made her eyeteeth stand out rather like a baby vampire's.

We progressed quickly to the eye test, which the girls failed, only because I was desperate to get them out of there and home where I felt they belonged.

"Do they know their alphabet yet?"

"Oh, yes," I declared honestly, with a great deal of relief. But when the nurse moved too far down the gym to hear them naming the letter cards she held up, things deteriorated. "This lady is very silly," Miguela advised in a stage whisper, and I knew neither of the girls would continue with the letter game. I began to improvise, which was unfortunate, since I had forgotten my glasses and couldn't see more than three feet past the end of my nose. After my third mistake, the children, who could both see and name letters, were ordered to have their eyes examined. Meekly, I agreed to take them. It was easier than explaining my own blindness and multiple misgivings about sending them out into this woman's world.

My fears that school would rob the girls of their individuality and spontaneity were put to rest early. It was Victoria Day, and on that cold evening, we sat huddled under blankets, watching "Poppy" light the fireworks. Miguela, always serious, looked on solemn-faced, while reflections of the Silver Cascade

her deep, dark eyes. Suddenly, fireworks lost their allu

tion, a big one, had formed in her mind. It was about N

godmother, and the brand new mother of a baby boy.

"Where did Tita Malaya get her baby from?" she asl

Lienne looked up at me, ready to learn. I wasn't su

I, were in the mood for the birds and the bees at this

moment. Hoping they might forget, I said, "We'll have

some day." Miguela returned to the fireworks, but

continued to think on the subject.

"You know, Mom. Some people make their own bal

people choose them."

"That's right," I said, happy we didn't have to go

depth than that for now.

"I'm only having one to start with. Babies one at a

don't want to make my baby, will you help me find or

"Sure," I said, feeling the buzz of monumental decisi

ing within my daughter. "But there's lots of time. You d

to decide right now. Look, there goes the Burning Scho

" 'Cause you choose good babies, don't you, Mom?"

"I choose the very nicest, most special ones," I said.

for her hand. Lienne squeezed my fingers and return

fireworks. The schoolhouse was a twinkling ember whe

Blue Rocket shot high into the air.

Then once more, as if to freeze her own special me

child turned to me with serious eyes. "These are the b

aren't they Mom?"

"They are," I answered. "The very best."

solemn-faced, while reflections of the Silver Cascade danced in her deep, dark eyes. Suddenly, fireworks lost their allure. A question, a big one, had formed in her mind. It was about Malaya, her godmother, and the brand new mother of a baby boy.

"Where did Tita Malaya get her baby from?" she asked.

Lienne looked up at me, ready to learn. I wasn't sure they, or I, were in the mood for the birds and the bees at this particular moment. Hoping they might forget, I said, "We'll have to ask her some day." Miguela returned to the fireworks, but her sister continued to think on the subject.

"You know, Mom. Some people make their own babies. Some people choose them."

"That's right," I said, happy we didn't have to go into more depth than that for now.

"I'm only having one to start with. Babies one at a time. If I don't want to make my baby, will you help me find one?"

"Sure," I said, feeling the buzz of monumental decisions forming within my daughter. "But there's lots of time. You don't have to decide right now. Look, there goes the Burning Schoolhouse."

"'Cause you choose good babies, don't you, Mom?"

"I choose the very nicest, most special ones," I said. I reached for her hand. Lienne squeezed my fingers and returned to the fireworks. The schoolhouse was a twinkling ember when the first Blue Rocket shot high into the air.

Then once more, as if to freeze her own special memory, my child turned to me with serious eyes. "These are the best times, aren't they Mom?"

"They are," I answered. "The very best."

"Your what, dear?" asked the lady, bending close to hear better.

Lienne began pointing at her crotch. "My moustache. I don't got one yet. It's coming later."

I pretended a trip to the bathroom was in order and hoped the woman was clever enough to move along to other things. When we got back, she was looking at Miguela, the way one might observe a potato beetle.

"Have the children been to the dentist yet?" she asked.

For some reason, known to her alone, Miguela chose that moment to stop scowling and smile one of her rare beatific smiles, revealing the four-tooth gap that made her eyeteeth stand out rather like a baby vampire's.

We progressed quickly to the eye test, which the girls failed, only because I was desperate to get them out of there and home where I felt they belonged.

"Do they know their alphabet yet?"

"Oh, yes," I declared honestly, with a great deal of relief. But when the nurse moved too far down the gym to hear them naming the letter cards she held up, things deteriorated. "This lady is very silly," Miguela advised in a stage whisper, and I knew neither of the girls would continue with the letter game. I began to improvise, which was unfortunate, since I had forgotten my glasses and couldn't see more than three feet past the end of my nose. After my third mistake, the children, who could both see and name letters, were ordered to have their eyes examined. Meekly, I agreed to take them. It was easier than explaining my own blindness and multiple misgivings about sending them out into this woman's world.

My fears that school would rob the girls of their individuality and spontaneity were put to rest early. It was Victoria Day, and on that cold evening, we sat huddled under blankets, watching "Poppy" light the fireworks. Miguela, always serious, looked on